TENDER IS THE NIGHT

The Broken Universe

TWAYNE'S MASTERWORK STUDIES

Robert Lecker, General Editor

TENDER IS THE NIGHT

The Broken Universe

Milton R. Stern

TWAYNE PUBLISHERS • NEW YORK
Maxwell Macmillan Canada • *Toronto*
Maxwell Macmillan International • *New York Oxford Singapore Sydney*

Twayne's Masterwork Studies No. 137

Twayne Publishers
Macmillan Publishing Company
866 Third Avenue
New York, New York 10022

Maxwell Macmillan Canada, Inc.
1200 Eglinton Avenue East
Suite 200
Don Mills, Ontario M3C 3N1

Library of Congress Cataloging-in-Publication Data

Stern, Milton R.
   Tender is the night : the broken universe / Milton R. Stern.
      p. cm.—(Twayne's masterworks studies; MWS 137)
   Includes bibliographical references and index.
   ISBN 0-8057-8380-6—ISBN 0-8057-8381-4 (pbk.)
   1. Fitzgerald, F. Scott (Francis Scott) 1896–1940. Tender is the Night. I. Title.
II. Series.
PS3511.I9T478 1994
813'.52—dc20
                                     93-40508
                                         CIP

Contents

Note on the References and Acknowledgments

It is both shameful and unbelievable that of the various carefully prepared editions of *Tender Is the Night,* there is no text of the book that is in print, carefully edited, final, *easily available,* and *inexpensive.* This is true for both the first-edition version and the revised version.

Although a majority of commentators favor the first-edition version, some of their arguments are weak and there are some very strong arguments supporting the "final" (as Fitzgerald termed it) revised version that Fitzgerald himself almost finished preparing before he died and that he very much wanted to publish. Because the revised version, edited by Malcolm Cowley (New York: Scribner's, 1951; reprinted by Scribner's in *Three Novels of F. Scott Fitzgerald,* 1953) has long been out of print, no easily useful citation can be made from that text at this writing. Although the first-edition version cited here (Scribner Library of Contemporary Classics, 1962), is, like all inexpensive, handily obtainable editions, a corrupt text, it is a paperback edition whose reprintings make it as easily and cheaply available as any on the market. Therefore, all page references to *Tender Is the Night* are to this text. Portions of this book are taken verbatim or in revised form from my introduction and my essay, "The Text Itself," in *Critical Essays on Fitzgerald's "Tender Is the Night,"* edited by Milton R. Stern, copyright © 1986 by Milton R. Stern, and are reprinted with permission of G. K. Hall, an imprint of Macmillan Publishing Company. The chapters that make up the second part of this volume, "A Reading," represent a revisiting of a reading of *Tender Is the Night* I had presented in *The Golden Moment.* Extended portions of these chapters are taken verba-

Note on the References and Acknowledgments

tim or in revised form from *The Golden Moment: The Novels of F. Scott Fitzgerald,* by Milton R. Stern (Urbana; University of Illinois Press, 1970), copyright © 1970 by the Board of Trustees of the University of Illinois, and are reprinted with permission of the University of Illinois Press.

F. Scott Fitzgerald
Photo by Carl Van Vechten. Courtesy of Scribners.

Chronology: F. Scott Fitzgerald's Life and Works

This chronology of Fitzgerald's life and works concludes with a brief history of the writing and publication of Tender Is the Night *between the years 1925 and 1934.*

1896   Named after one of his father's illustrious ancestors, Francis Scott Key Fitzgerald is born on 24 September in St. Paul, Minnesota, to Edward and Mary ("Molly") McQuillan Fitzgerald.

1898   Economic necessity moves the family to Buffalo, New York.

1901   The same necessity moves them again, this time to Syracuse, New York. His father's distinguished heritage brings no money; his mother's family money brings no distinction. At a very young age Fitzgerald becomes acutely conscious of an intimate connection between American identity, money, and social position. In July Scott's sister, Annabel, is born.

1903   And yet once more: back to Buffalo. For Scott the names of towns in upstate New York, like Herkimer, are to become metaphors for failed dreams.

1908   Economic problems move the family back to St. Paul. Scott is enrolled in the socially estimable St. Paul Academy.

1911   Enters Newman School, a private Catholic high school in New Jersey. Already sees himself as a playwright and story writer.

1913   Enters his dream school, Princeton, class of 1917.

1914   World War I begins. The young Princetonian meets and falls in love with Ginevra King, a beautiful young social queen of great Chicago wealth that makes her unavailable to him. She remains a metaphor for Fitzgerald's golden girl.

1915   Drops out of Princeton in his junior year. His concentration on extracurricular dramatic productions of the Triangle Club and on his social affairs results in academic failure.

1916   Reenrolls at Princeton as a member of the class of 1918. He will enter the army and never graduate.

1917   In April the United States enters the war; in November the USSR is established. Fitzgerald takes officer's training as a second lieutenant at Fort Leavenworth, Kansas. Begins writing his first novel while in the army.

1918   Completes first draft of *The Romantic Egotist,* which will be rejected, but with encouragement, by Scribner's. Is transferred to Camp Sheridan, near Montgomery, Alabama, where he meets Zelda, daughter of an Alabama supreme court Justice. She is the golden girl of the young officers at Camp Sheridan. Fitzgerald falls in love with her. In November World War I ends, finishing his romantic dreams of wartime glory.

1919   Having become engaged to Zelda, and now discharged from the army, Fitzgerald leaves Alabama and goes to New York to seek literary greatness. Begins by working in an advertising agency while he rewrites *The Romantic Egotist,* which he will rename *The Education of a Personage.* This too will, with encouragement, be rejected by Scribner's. But in the spring the *Smart Set* accepts his first commercial story, "Babes in the Woods." In June, impatient about waiting for Fitzgerald to become a success, Zelda breaks her engagement to him. Fitzgerald holes up at his parents' home in St. Paul to stake everything on the success of another rewrite of his novel. Changes the title again: *This Side of Paradise.* In September Scribner's accepts *This Side of Paradise,* expecting a marketplace success. In October Fitzgerald sells "Head and Shoulders" to the *Saturday Evening Post,* beginning a long and lucrative literary relationship with that extremely popular slick. He begins a successful career of selling steadily to the top-paying magazines. In November his engagement to Zelda is reestablished, teaching him once more that nothing succeeds like success in winning the golden girl.

1920   In March *This Side of Paradise* is published and is an immediate hit. In April Scott and Zelda marry; move to Westport, Connecticut; and begin a glamorous and self-destructive life. Scribner's follows each of Fitzgerald's novels with a collection of his short stories. The first of these, *Flappers and Philosophers,* is published in September, and in October the Fitzgeralds move to Manhattan.

Chronology

1921   The Fitzgeralds take their first trip to Europe, where Scott vibrates to expatriate excitement as he observes the new playground for American money. Returning, the Fitzgeralds move to St. Paul for recuperative peace and quiet and the birth of their daughter, Scottie.

1922   Scott's second novel, *The Beautiful and Damned,* and the second volume of short stories, *Tales of the Jazz Age,* are published. Scott gives the Jazz Age its name. The Fitzgeralds move to Great Neck, Long Island, where Scott soaks up setting for *The Great Gatsby.*

1923   Fitzgerald returns to an early love, the drama, working on a play called *The Vegetable; or, from President to Postman. The Vegetable* is published in April, produced in November, and flops at once.

1924   The Fitzgeralds move abroad and in the summer meet Gerald and Sara Murphy, who represent to Scott both the responsible idealism of an older America and the American experience of Europe in the Jazz Age. (*Tender Is the Night* is dedicated "To Gerald and Sara / Many Fetes.") Benito Mussolini fully consolidates power in Italy, stirring antifascist sentiments in Fitzgerald.

1925   *The Great Gatsby* is published. The Fitzgeralds move to Paris; in the Dingo Bar Scott and Ernest Hemingway meet for the first time. Scott had championed the hitherto unknown writer and continues supportive praise. He begins the first of several versions of what is to become *Tender Is the Night.*

1926   Zelda shows signs of possibly psychotic behavior. The third collection of short stories, *All the Sad Young Men,* is published, and in February the Fitzgeralds move back to the Côte d'Azur, where they rent villas at Juan-les-Pins for the rest of the year. In December they return to America.

1927   Scott goes to Hollywood for the first time, working for United Artists, and begins with the movie industry a complex relationship of scorn, failure, and financial dependence. He is attracted to the young movie star Lois Moran (more material for *Tender Is the Night:* Rosemary Hoyt). In March the Fitzgeralds move to Ellerslie, an estate near Wilmington, Delaware. Zelda begins her ballet passion.

1928   The *Saturday Evening Post* publishes the first of the Basil Duke Lee stories. During the summer in Paris, Zelda increasingly displays abnormal behavior in her desire to become a ballerina.

The Fitzgeralds return to Ellerslie in search of unfound peace.

1929   Back to Europe again: Italy, Paris, and Cannes once more. The stock market crashes in October: the end of the Jazz Age and of "the greatest, gaudiest spree in history."

1930   In Paris Zelda suffers a severe breakdown and is hospitalized in French and Swiss clinics. The Great Depression begins in earnest, personally in every sense in the Fitzgeralds' life, and nationally in American life. The *Saturday Evening Post* publishes the first of the Josephine stories. Zelda enters the Prangins clinic outside Geneva, Switzerland. Events thus immerse Scott in the raw materials of *Tender Is the Night*.

1931 Scott returns to the United States to attend his father's funeral: more Dick Diver material for *Tender Is the Night*. Zelda is released from Prangins, and the Fitzgeralds move back to America for good. In search of emotional stability, they live in Zelda's hometown of Montgomery, Alabama. In December Scott tries another foray in Hollywood, this time at Metro-Goldwyn-Mayer.

1932   Zelda breaks down a second time and enters Phipps clinic in the Johns Hopkins Hospital, Baltimore. Fitzgerald moves to Towson, Maryland, near Baltimore, and rents "La Paix." By now that name is tragically ironic for both Scott and Zelda, who will rejoin her husband and daughter there. Zelda's *Save Me the Waltz* is published in October.

1933   Nazi Germany is established as Hitler becomes Chancellor. Finances dictate that the Fitzgeralds give up La Paix and move to Park Avenue in Baltimore, where, within a month, Zelda will experience a third breakdown.

1934   Zelda enters Sheppard-Pratt Hospital. She will spend most of the rest of her life institutionalized. On 11 April *Tender Is the Night* is published.

1935   With intermittent stays in Baltimore and New York, Scott moves to North Carolina (Tryon, Hendersonville, but primarily Asheville), where he will remain for two years writing and living his "Crack-Up" pieces. The fourth postnovel collection of short stories, aptly titled *Taps at Reveille,* is published.

1936   Zelda is committed to Highland Hospital, Asheville, where, except for occasional visits, she will live until her death by fire when her wing of the hospital burns down in March 1948. From 1936 until his death, Scott attempts to arrange republication of *Tender Is the Night* and he continues to work on what he calls the "final," revised version. In September his mother dies.

1937   Financially desperate, Scott moves to Hollywood as a scriptwriter for MGM and meets Sheilah Graham during the summer. While working as a scriptwriter he also continues to produce his own fiction. His MGM contract is renewed for a year.

1938   Fitzgerald moves about (Encino, Malibu Beach), desperately writing scripts and magazine fiction to meet his bills. His MGM contract is not renewed.

1939   Fitzgerald's catastrophic drunken trip to Hanover, New Hampshire, to work with Budd Schulberg on the script of a movie about the Dartmouth Winter Carnival for Walter Wanger. In 1939 and 1940 Fitzgerald freelances for Columbia, MGM, Paramount, Twentieth Century–Fox, and Universal. In September Nazi Germany invades Poland, and World War II begins. Fitzgerald begins work on *The Last Tycoon*. Unfinished when he died, *The Last Tycoon* fragment displays all of his artistic brilliance and gives every promise that it would have been the great American Hollywood novel. Fitzgerald also begins to write rushed short pieces about a sleazy Hollywood scriptwriter named Pat Hobby.

1940   Begins publishing the Pat Hobby stories. Once commanding $4,200 per story from the *Saturday Evening Post*, Fitzgerald, ignored and all but forgotten, sells the Pat Hobby pieces to *Esquire* for $250 each. He moves, for the last time, to 1403 North Laurel Avenue, Hollywood. In November he has his first heart attack. In December he dies, in Sheilah Graham's apartment, of a second heart attack, without completing all of his revisions for *Tender Is the Night*.

1925–1934   In the fall of 1925 Fitzgerald begins "the Melarkey version" of *Tender Is the Night*: the protagonist is a young man named Francis Melarkey. Between 1925 and 1930 this version undergoes five revisions, variously titled *Our Type, The World's Fair, The Melarkey Case,* and *The Boy Who Killed His Mother.* In the summer of 1929 Francis Fitzgerald abandons Francis Melarkey and begins anew with a protagonist named Lew Kelly, a movie director whose wife is named Nicole. "The Kelly version," a sixth revision of the novel, never gets beyond the beginning, but it introduces a hopeful starlet named Rosemary. In the spring of 1930 Fitzgerald returns to the Melarkey version, but Zelda's breakdowns, Hollywood, changes of address, and other problems delay continued work. In the spring of 1932 Scott merges the materials of the previous rewrites. In the course of the various revisions and versions, characters named Seth and Dinah Roreback emerge, evolve into Seth and Dinah Piper, and then into Dick and Nicole Diver. A character named Abe Herkimer evolves into Abe Grant and then into Abe North. Fitzgerald will work on six revisions of "the Diver version," variously titling it *The Drunkard's Holiday, Dr. Diver's Holiday,* and *Richard Diver.* In October 1933 the manuscript finally goes to Scribner's, and in November Fitzgerald changes the title to *Tender Is the Night,* borrowing a line from Keats's "Ode to a Nightingale." From January to April 1934, the novel runs in serial form in *Scribner's Magazine.* After seven rewrites of the Diver version, from first notes through revisions on galley proofs, Fitzgerald writes a continuing eighth revision of the Diver version on the page proofs of the four monthly installments of the serial publication. He revises the magazine version again on galleys for the book and yet again on page proofs for the book. Finally, after three versions comprising 17 revisions, Fitzgerald publishes the book on 11 April 1934. Thereafter he works sporadically on a structural eighteenth revision, retelling the story in a straight chronological development of Dick Diver's career, but he does not live to complete the last details of the final version he wishes to publish.

LITERARY AND
HISTORICAL CONTEXT

1

War and Grace: The Importance of *Tender Is the Night*

F. Scott Fitzgerald had been born into a Victorian era that emphasized stiff proprieties and the initiation of the young into the seemly traditions and decorous conventions of a prim nineteenth-century world: chastity, conformist nationalism and religiosity, polite manners and language, prissy public values and behavior. But he grew up in a rebellious era, following World War I, in which all the old gods and proprieties had been demolished in the high explosive disillusion and cynicism occasioned by the unspeakable carnage and conditions of the Great War. If the war and its aftermath were the heritage of all the noble rhetoric and repressive prissiness of proper society, then, reasoned the new generation, proper society be damned. During the 1920s the hemlines of young women's dresses went up and up. The beat of dance music went down and dirty into jazz. Speakeasies, hipflasks, home brew, and political corruption made a mockery of Prohibition, and the careers of gangsters vied with those of sports heroes for public admiration in the popular culture. To the shocked and bewildered elders, who still lived in the Victorian far side of World War I, whose common cultural connection with their children was strained and often broken, and who knew that the world was going to hell in a handbasket, the new generation was one of reprehensibly "flaming youth."

Fitzgerald was aware of the total cultural exhaustion of the Victorian world of his parents, yet he was also aware that the context of that world was one in which identities, expectations, and society had been relatively stable, one in which the world had seemed a reliable and predictable place. As he always did, Fitzgerald used biographical experience as metaphors for cultural context. Into the makings of *Tender Is the Night,* Fitzgerald imaginatively blended his father's life and family history as the impoverished end of a distinguished line that had devolved to outworn gentilities; but Fitzgerald was also aware of the vitality and revolutionary heroism out of which the family had grown. In his view of the demise of that nobility, Fitzgerald saw his father's world of good manners as a lingering representation of decency, dignity, and honor, a dim nineteenth-century memory of what, in the heroic beginnings of the American nation, had been seen as humankind's most exciting hope of a noble, new history. In Fitzgerald's imaginative and evocative examinations of the American experience, decency, dignity, honor, energy, work, dependability, and hope became merged with the far American past—a myth, a dream, the transcendent energy and vision of an America that at one time had existed as an imagined and infinitely hope-filled country of the heart and spirit. In *Tender Is the Night* Dick Diver reminisces that "his father had been sure of what he was, with a deep pride of the two proud widows who had raised him to believe that nothing could be superior to 'good instincts,' honor, courtesy, and courage" (204).

But the young Scott Fitzgerald was just as intensely aware of the other face of the American heritage, an actuality of hypocrisy, coarseness, cynicism, and greed that was the postwar legacy of the world of the fathers, the destructive corruption of the dream. That aspect of Fitzgerald's imagination also went back into the past, into a discovery that the America of the dream had never existed, that however far back we travel or widely we range in the history of human affairs, the members of the human race, including Americans, always have been fallen creatures. What was important and glorious, Fitzgerald learned as he traveled through the history and geography of his American imagination, was the dreaming itself. What identified the dream, the *idea* of America, was the youthful vitality and optimism, the old certainty, like Jay Gatsby's, that time could be remade, that the world could be redeemed, that a condition of bliss that transcended past experience could be achieved.

The idea of America was no less than the perennial vision of redemption that has always existed as various myths in the collective, yearning vision of the entire human race. The phrase "the American Dream" has degenerated almost into meaninglessness through overgeneral popular usage and through the sloppy, overabundant, witless rhetoric of politicians, editorialists, and advertisers. When there is a clearly discernible meaning, the phrase generally has deteriorated into indicating upward social and economic mobility: having a lot, being secure, belonging—in a word, money. But for Fitzgerald it was far more. The idea of America was "a willingness of the heart," as he phrased it in a short story, "The Swimmers," a response to a dream of unrestricted being, a vision of freedom that allowed the exercise of the most transcendent imagination. That vision was essentially religious. It was nothing less than absolute belief in the absolute redemption of history since the Fall, centered on fulfillment of the endless possibilities of the aspiring individual self. The New World would literally usher in a new world. Dick Diver, the man who would cure insane, war-torn history and reclaim the world from the sickness bequeathed by the legacy of the elders, believed no less than Jay Gatsby in the millennial promise of the fresh, green, beckoning new world. All of Fitzgerald's heroes share excitement and belief in the certainty of that promise. And all of them come to learn that humans live in history, not in absolute redemption of or from the past. Even at the joyous beginning of his career, in his second book, *The Beautiful and Damned* (1922), Fitzgerald had centered his characters on his recognition of mortal doom and the self-deceptions and illusions of a Jazz Age generation of flaming youth who thought the bright fire would never die.

Fitzgerald recognized his own Jazz Age gorgeous moment as a brief American idyll that turned out to be a sordid corruption of its own promise. "It's odd that my talent for the short story vanished," he wrote wistfully to Zelda two months before he died. "It was partly that times changed, editors changed, but part of it was tied up somehow with you and me—the happy ending."[1] As he summed up the matter in one of his moving letters to Scottie, "[M]y generation of radicals and breakers-down never found anything to take the place of the old virtues of work and courage and the old graces of courtesy and politeness" (July 1938, *Letters*, 36).

In Fitzgerald's vision (as in the vision of many historians) World War I marked a breaking point in American history and in Western history generally. And in that breaking point Fitzgerald saw profoundly into a tragic inversion. Before World War I, there was the young America. The *young* America, paradoxically, was the old America, back there in the past when the American world was young. The postwar *new* America, however, was no longer the redeemer nation, but was very much part of the old, international, corrupt actuality of history that had eventually burst forth in the sickness of World War I. The new generation that emerged from the war became in Fitzgerald's vision metaphoric material for everything that always had been selfishly irresponsible and greedily self-gratifying in the same old, tired world—and in American life. He saw the affluent, fun-filled Roaring Twenties as the coarse diminishment of the American Dream, not its fulfillment. In Fitzgerald's historical imagination the history of manners becomes a cultural clue to the meaning, the moral development, of an era. An entire civilization can be tested and evaluated in the values that surround what it does to the hero of the novel. Fitzgerald thought of *Tender Is the Night* as his *Vanity Fair*, even calling it *The World's Fair* in one draft.

In the educational canon that young Scott took from his schooling, a holdover from the world of his parents, he found in the Romantic poets, especially in Keats, the dramatic postures of betrayed, suffering, heroic youth struggling to break free from the trammels of a cruelly fallen world. In Keats he found not only attitudes, but language. After one reads Keats, he once wrote his daughter, all other poetry seems like mere "humming" (3 August 1940, *Letters*, 88). Fitzgerald's literary quest was an attempt to combine contemporary tendencies toward sophisticated, hardboiled style, especially as it came to be manifested in the detective novel and the proletarian fiction of the 1930s, with the Keatsian luxuriance of Romantic style.

A consideration of style involves a matter too rich and complex to be dealt with here in any but a summary way, and that matter is modernism. The stylistic essence of modernism was a repudiation of Victorian formality and rhetorical lushness, a disenchanted disavowal of traditional and conventional views of experience and methods of expression, an experimentalist search for the kind of form that pared everything down to structural essentials, and an effort to produce the essentials of *impression* created by representative details of experience. Modernism paradoxically became at once objective and personal, relentlessly realistic and intensely subjective in its search for space and color relationships, space and mass relationships, tone and time relationships, word and meaning relationships that would express the artist's perceptions of reality in new forms. A large part of modernism was the attempt to merge the inner, associational impression of things with the precisely rendered *image* that captures the impression—exactly as in Impressionist painting—thereby rendering consciousness, or human reality, into art forms.

The manner was well suited to the disillusion of the postwar period. The revolutionary experimentalism of modernism was the intellectual dimension of the Jazz Age generation that Fitzgerald chronicled. In his inclinations, values, style, and historical sense Fitzgerald was a child and exponent of modernism. When the "flaming youth" of the 1920s proclaimed him their spokesman and the genius of his time, they recognized in his prose—which, unlike the baffling and frustrating newness of much modernist art, was accessible to them—the instincts of their modernist age. But at the same time, in his inclinations, values, style, and historical sense, Fitzgerald was also a conservative compelled by what he saw as precious in aspects of the past. In Dick Diver he championed what he defined as civilized morality in that area where Victorian politeness and Romantic aspiration merged in a responsible and imaginative individual.

When he was writing the novel in the grim bleakness of the 1930s, Fitzgerald was aware of the anachronism of such an individual. With the wintry persistence of the decade's cold economic actualities, realism emerged more and more as a narrative mode, ever present in what came to be called proletarian literature. Thus, the ways in which the *dis*illusioning Great Depression helped shape modernism developed another nexus between Fitzgerald and his American predecessors such as Twain and Crane, bringing him into a line of development with all the realists and naturalists who emerged in American literature after the Civil War.

In addition to modernism, the historical context also included Oswald Spengler, whose *Decline of the West,* although translated from the original German into English too late (1926) for Fitzgerald to have read while he was writing *The Great Gatsby* (published in 1925)—had become a staple of intellectual diet in America at least four years before *Gatsby.* In rhythm with Wagnerian cycles in which the very gods decline, Spengler envisioned the end of the energy cycle of Western civilization, and World War I did much to give strong credence and currency to his ideas among the flaming youth, intellectual or otherwise, rebelliously emerging into the 1920s. Further, the essence of the Romanticism in which Fitzgerald had read was change, rebellion, the dissolution of the old.

Moreover, in the 1920s and 1930s the popular versions of Freud—what came to be referred to with facile profundity as "Freudianism"—appeared. For good and for ill, psychology and psychiatry became major materials for literary use. The historical fact that Zelda Fitzgerald's descent into psychosis was coincident with the popularization of the new study of psychology merely allowed certain givens for *Tender Is the Night.* Although cheap and sensationalistic fictions exploiting emotional problems blinded some critics to the true value of *Tender Is the Night,* Fitzgerald never paddled in the literary shallows where mawkish or lurid uses of psychology were made by hacks. Too much of his heart and soul were profoundly involved in Zelda's tragedy, too much deep love and high feeling, too much invincible artistry for hack-work. The subject matter of abnormal psychology, refined in the alembic of Fitzgerald's creative imagination, emerged from the raw grief of his life in *Tender Is the Night* not as sensationalistic stuff, but as a magnificently and complexly wrought metaphor for the American history handed down by the generations and for his own version of the decline of the West.

Freud and Spengler were not the only German intellectuals to add yeast to the turmoil of feelings and ideas that followed World War I. Karl Marx, although earlier than either (he died in 1883), became a posthumous force to be reckoned with, especially after the Russian Revolution. In America Marxist ideas became widespread during the Great Depression, the decade of the 1930s in which Fitzgerald was completing *Tender Is the Night*. Although he was hardly a Marxist, Fitzgerald sometimes thought of himself as one and occasionally referred to himself as one, even insisting that his daughter read the chapter on the working day in *Das Kapital*. Like Freudianism and Spenglerian thought, Marxism intensified the postwar repudiation of the old manners and morals as frippery that had veiled reality and that was an expression of old privileges and castes and identities that were dying in the tumultuous birth of a new generation. In *Tender Is the Night* the distaste with which Fitzgerald views the appearances of wealth and power—whether in the representatives of international wealth, in the nighttime adornment of the American ambassador in Rome, or in the fact that the Warrens' American wealth and power end up wedded to militaristic adventurers like Tommy Barban—indicates the effect of the times on Fitzgerald's consciousness.

In accounting for the historical context of *Tender Is the Night*, one finds that the personal dimensions of biographical fact are as pertinent as the intellectual influences. Fitzgerald always used actual people and personal events as the raw materials out of which he made a composite for his basic themes. Even more than for Fitzgerald's preceding books, it would be possible to make an almost complete list of the many items of one-to-one correspondence between the Fitzgeralds' lives (especially during the two and one half years abroad between mid-1924 and late 1926) and the novel. It was inevitable that early reviewers and Fitzgerald's friends and acquaintances should have seen the novel as disguised autobiography, a judgment reinforced by Fitzgerald's use of "composite" characters.[2] Even as late as the 1950s some commentators continued to see *Tender Is the Night* rather narrowly as fictional autobiography, "a documentary of the novelist's own collapse."[3] Only a few reviewers saw the unlucky novel in its true dimensions. Those dimensions are enormous, for Fitzgerald made his novel—his "testament of faith"[4] in his greatest abilities and in the importance of creating literature—something much wider than a fictitious documentary of his own experience as an individual. As Fitzgerald's life and times move farther into the past, we move very quickly from the biographical specifics of the historical context to Fitzgerald's process of compositing the materials.

To take one example, we find that we cannot dismiss Abe North, for instance, simply by saying that he was based on Fitzgerald's friend, the writer Ring Lardner (as, in part, he was). In his obituary essay, "Ring," Fitzgerald makes unmistakable his own sense of Lardner's essential Americanness. In developing Abe out of Lardner, Fitzgerald uses some of Lardner's characteristics to create quite explicitly a hint of Lincoln and the Civil War. Abe's "voice was slow and shy; he had one of the saddest faces Rosemary had ever seen, the high cheek bones of an Indian, a long upper lip, and enormous deep-set golden eyes" (9). But when this ruined "Lincoln" becomes involved with black people—significantly, with a man named *Freeman*—the result is not emancipation, but murder.

In the book's pervasive metaphor of war, Fitzgerald uses the Civil War as he uses World War I—as an end to innocence, an end to the days of old graces and virtues dissolved into the corruption associated with the administration of President U. S. Grant, who also had been so full of promise as a young general. So Abe, the "factual" Ring Lardner, is also the "factual" U. S. (perfect initials!) Grant. In fact, in one version, before Fitzgerald gave Abe the last name of North, Abe's last name had been Grant. A man of promise, North "was a musician who, after a brilliant and precocious start had composed nothing for seven years" (34). As he began the completion of *Tender Is the Night,* Fitzgerald felt that he had composed nothing serious in the seven years since *The Great Gatsby.* "Grant," like Dan (read: Buffalo Bill) Cody in *The Great Gatsby,* becomes a name for early personal as well as national promise, and also for the debauchery of that promise. So too, the early, promising Dick Diver, ready to begin his moment, is likened to "Grant, lolling in his general store in Galena, . . . ready to be called to an intricate destiny" (118). Talking about the battles fought in the World War I trenches that Dick's party visits, Abe says, "General Grant invented this kind of battle at Petersburg in sixty-five." But Dick's reply introduces the other side of the brilliant early promise: "No he didn't," Dick answers, "—he just invented mass butchery" (57). Abe, in the depths of the drunkenness that results in the murder of a black man, likens himself to Grant in his debauchery: "But remember what George the Third said, that if Grant was drunk he wished he would bite the other generals" (108). And just as Dick's career opened, like that of the triumphant general, on a note of promise, so it ironically closes: Nicole liked to think that Dick's career was still "biding its time, again like Grant's in Galena" (315).

The gradual and increasing degeneration and destruction of Abe are a complete foreshadowing of what happens to the young promise embodied in Dick. Abe is savagely beaten in a drunken brawl and he crawls away to die. Dick is beaten insensible in a drunken brawl with the police. Abe is a paradigm of Dick as Grant is of them both, and as Lincoln is of all the national and international tragedy of a great historical promise lost. Fitzgerald uses Abe as a prefiguration of the demise of Dick Diver, archetypal American savior. The theme of the book becomes history itself, the Spenglerian process of the collapse of a civilization into barbarism as we watch a healer who represents the best of an entire nation paradigmatically collapse into oblivion.[5] In short, the actual Ring Lardner "fact" of Abe North is a biographical certainty in any discussion of the historical contexts and dimensions of Fitzgerald's book. But the fact itself is much less important than Fitzgerald's use of it, and in this introduction to the historical context of *Tender Is the Night* Abe North serves as just one highly representative example of Fitzgerald's use of the details of biographical and historical context.

In a letter to Scribner's great editor, Maxwell Perkins, the impoverished Scott Fitzgerald pleaded for the possibility of a reprinting of *The Great Gatsby* as one more title in a series of 25-cent paperbacks. "Would a popular reissue," he asked, "with a preface *not* by me but by one of my admirers—I can maybe pick one—make it a favorite with classrooms, profs, lovers of English prose—anybody? But to die, so completely and unjustly after having given so much! Even now there is little published in American fiction that doesn't slightly bear my stamp—in a *small* way I was an original" (20 May 1940, *Letters*, 288).

The pathos of such pleading is equaled only by the painfulness of a vision of F. Scott Fitzgerald reduced to such a diminished view of himself by adversity and literary oblivion, for he was certainly an original. He introduced the idea of an entire generation in recoil and rebellion, a theme and a set of materials that since his focus on them in American fiction have been echoed again and again by the antiheroes of post–World War II fiction of the 1940s and 1950s, by the beat generation of the 1950s and 1960s, by the hip generation of the 1960s and 1970s, and by every dissenting generational sense that has transcribed itself in American fiction from Norman Mailer to J. D. Salinger to Ken Kesey to the present moment. Before Fitzgerald the literature of dissent was not so much an identification of generations as it was a struggle of the individual against self, society, and the universe. The pioneering experimentalists in realism and naturalism and literary impressionism—Fitzgerald's literary predecessors—were concerned more with universal types of the human psyche alone amid forces than with the historical identification of generations.

Fitzgerald changed that. In a *large* way he was an original. Not only in his marriage of Romanticism, realism, and modernism, but also in his subject matter he introduced new directions in American literature (for instance, he was one of the first to see Hollywood as archetypal American material), discovering that by turning his characters into generations, in effect, he could articulate his moral and historical vision of the meaning of American experience in the changes of time. And nowhere more than in *Tender Is the Night* did Fitzgerald successfully adapt his prose style to the metaphoric creation of the moral history of America. No other book so fully as *Tender Is the Night* becomes *the* American historical novel, in which the *idea* of America, the idealized and idealizing promises of the past, and its loss are identified and defined against the background of the disillusioning actualities of the present generation.[6]

War and Grace

American history (especially the Civil War and World War I), the Russian Revolution, the rise and fall of the Jazz Age, Zelda Fitzgerald's mental illness, the rise of fascism, the Great Depression, Hollywood scriptwriting, modernism, Imagism, Impressionism, symbolism, realism, Marxism, Freudianism, women's liberation and sexual identity, Spenglerian thought, and personal experience representative of the times all form the historical context of *Tender Is the Night*. They all went into the making of Fitzgerald's feel of a personal, national, and international dying Fall from Grace. He renders the vulgarity of a spiritually crippled world that characterizes itself in the fact that it has no sense of what it is losing in the decline of Dr. Richard Diver. With the sapping of Dick's vitality and the destruction of Diver's gifts Fitzgerald sums up the personal and historical contexts of his time in *Tender Is the Night*. The story is a vastly rich moral account of the twentieth-century Western world's entire history, in which its last, best hope—its archetypal American and the "old" America of youthful dream—is drained, used up, and thrown away.

2

Hostile Was the Night:
Critical Issues and Reception

Tender Is the Night had to wait too many years for its completion. Fitzgerald had worked on it off and on for almost nine years before it was published. Then it had to wait 17 more years for the posthumous publication of the final revised version Fitzgerald had longed for. And despite some strong commentaries in its behalf, it had to wait approximately a quarter-century after its original publication for full and general recognition of its value in any version.

Every student of Fitzgerald's work is familiar with Hemingway's remark that the "strange thing is that in retrospect his *Tender Is the Night* gets better and better."[1] The observation is a paradigm and encapsulation of critical attention. When Alexander Cowie published his historical survey of the American novel eight years after Fitzgerald's death, he spared only a one sentence reference to F. Scott Fitzgerald, a comment on *This Side of Paradise*.[2] And even in that, Fitzgerald had to share equal billing with Percy Marks, a minor writer whose works, especially *The Plastic Age,* belong to the "littered Five-and-Ten" (196) of mind and materials that Fitzgerald had shopped in for *This Side of Paradise*. In 1963, when Arthur Mizener, who early championed *Tender Is the Night* as Fitzgerald's most brilliant novel,[3] published *F. Scott Fitzgerald: A Collection of Critical Essays,*[4] even Mizener allowed only one entry for *Tender Is the Night*—a 1934 review.[5] And as late as 1973, in Kenneth E. Eble's collection, *F. Scott Fitzgerald: A Collection of Criticism,*[6] there are three essays on *The Great Gatsby,* five on special topics, and one apiece for *This Side of Paradise, The Beautiful and Damned, The Last Tycoon* fragment—and *Tender Is the Night.* This neglect of *Tender Is the Night* resulted partly from the fact that through the 1950s some of the best observations about the book existed in general considerations of Fitzgerald rather than in criticism that concentrated on the novel itself (of which there was relatively little). In fact, in 1969, when the first collection of essays on *Tender Is the Night* appeared,[7] one-fifth of the inclusions comprised general essays rather than concentrations on the novel. Attention to the novel was spurred by the two appearances of the revised version (1951 and 1953), but it took almost two decades after Fitzgerald's death for critics to realize how much "better and better" *Tender Is the Night* became.

THE 1930s

Most of the reviews in the 1930s placed *Tender Is the Night* in one of three categories, few reviewers acknowledging more than one: (1) a study of abnormal psychology growing out of the fashionable triumph of "Freudianism"; (2) a study of domestic disquiet, a "marriage novel"; and (3) yet one more Fitzgerald tale of glamorous, decadent Jazz Age playboys and -girls, and, worse yet, in the outworn mode (yawn) of expatriation. Whatever the reviewers' classifications of theme, their objections tended to reiterate two observations: (1) there was no convincing—or at least clear—reason for Dick's disintegration, and (2) the shift in point of view and chronology after the Rosemary beginning was confusing.

These classifications seem now to offer the interest of an anti-quarian's curiosities, for the novel has far outgrown the limitations placed on it by most of the early reviewers. The question of rich expatriate jazzbabies as subject matter for readers burdened by the Great Depression, however, requires a bit more attention. Some of the Depression-era reviews were intensely political (Philip Rahv's *Daily Worker* essay, "You Can't Duck Hurricane under a Beach Umbrella" is a strong example)[8] and took Fitzgerald to task for being stubbornly retrogressive in ignoring contemporary economics and the rise of fascism. Although not all the reviews picked up this note, several did. The reviews that followed Malcolm Cowley's 1951 edition of *Tender Is the Night,* and then again after the 1953 *Three Novels of F. Scott Fitzgerald*—both published by Scribner's—created the impression that leftist political reviews like Philip Rahv's accounted for the failure of the novel and for Fitzgerald's desire to revise it. Malcolm Cowley's introduction to the revised version influentially strengthened that impression: "*Tender* . . . dealt with fashionable life in the 1920s at a time when most readers wanted to forget that they had ever been concerned with frivolities; the new fashion was for novels about destitution and revolt" (*Tender,* in *Three Novels,* iv).

In the 1960s Bruccoli's *The Composition of "Tender Is the Night"*[9] attempted a corrective for this assumption. This corrective had been anticipated by Charles Poore in 1951[10] and was consolidated by Bruccoli in "*Tender Is the Night*—Reception and Reputation":

> But it is not demonstrable that Fitzgerald was the victim of a hostile, New Deal oriented press. In all fairness, the assassination of *Tender Is the Night* cannot be added to the catalogue of Democrats' iniquities. . . . A glance at the ten best-selling novels of 1934 provides nothing to suggest that the readers of the Depression rejected Fitzgerald because they preferred socially significant novels about slums: *Anthony Adverse; Lamb in His Bosom; So Red the Rose; Good-bye, Mr. Chips; Within This Present; Work of Art; Private Worlds; Mary Peters; Oil for the Lamps of China;* and *Seven Gothic Tales.* This is a typical mixture, and there is not one proletarian novel in the lot. Indeed, *Within this Present* is a nostalgic look back at the twenties . . . the three top sellers of the year were historical novels. . . . People who lament the failure of *Tender Is the Night* generally ignore the fact

that Fitzgerald had not had a best seller since *This Side of Paradise,* and even it was not one of the top ten in 1920. Fitzgerald was a popular figure, but he was never really a popular novelist in his lifetime.[11]

The corrective itself, however, requires a slight correction.[12] For one thing, Fitzgerald did not think of *Tender Is the Night* as popular fiction subject to the standards of dime-store bestsellerdom. He was entirely wrapped up in it as the great work that would be his bid for removal from the ranks of popular romancers and for placement among the lasting, serious artists. For another, the more intellectual journals—like *Harper's,* the *Atlantic,* and the *Saturday Review of Literature* among wide-circulation magazines, and like the *Modern Monthly* among smaller periodicals,[13] did not pay the kind of attention to popular bestseller fare that they did to books they took seriously. To a large extent Fitzgerald *was* identified among serious readers with Jazz Age parties and expatriates, and serious readers and serious journals were seriously involved with serious matters of serious world politics and the serious Depression. The reviews that tended to classify *Tender Is the Night* into categories of subject matter—and most of them did—did not encourage consideration of the novel by serious readers. C. Hartley Grattan's review[14] was one of the few appreciative notices that cut across easy categories and hinted at the dimensions of the novel. It is not insignificant that Fitzgerald wrote to the Marxist critic, George Goetz, who used the pseudonym V. F. Calverton for his own books and his editorship of the *Modern Monthly,* that "Grattan's review in the *Modern Monthly* . . . pleased me more than any I got."[15] Moreover, Fitzgerald, like most of his literary contemporaries, was at least mildly sympathetic to politically conscious, Left-leaning positions in the 1930s, both while writing *Tender Is the Night* and then when reading reviews of it. In sum, although Bruccoli's corrective is necessary, there remains more justification than Bruccoli allows for Cowley's assumption about the effect—the general context and ambience—of the reviews of the 1930s on Fitzgerald and on the sales of *Tender Is the Night.* The nature of the bestsellers in 1934 does not account for the special nature of *Tender Is the Night* in 1934. There were both praise and condemnation for the book from commercial popular reviewers as well as from the intelligentsia. But the ill-starred book was too serious a piece of literature to enter the ranks of popular light reading, and the categorizing receptions generated by its setting and materials denied it compensatory enthusiasm from highbrow sources. Given the context of the times, the atmosphere, and the sense Fitzgerald had of his book and his own politics, the political responses were in fact consequential for Fitzgerald and for the reception of *Tender Is the Night*.

But when we turn to two other major objections raised by the reviews of the 1930s—the mysteriousness of Dick's destruction and a structural confusion of point of view occasioned by the switch of focus from Rosemary to Dick—Bruccoli is closer to the mark than Cowley.[16] In his introduction to the revised version, Cowley suggests that "in spite of knowing so much about . . . [Dick], we are never quite certain of the reasons for his decline."[17] Nevertheless, the quantity and variety of criticism in the 1960s and 1970s abundantly indicate that in either the original or the revised version readers have no trouble identifying what Fitzgerald had made dramatically clear. On the level of psychology and personality, Dick contained the inner flaws of his nation's transcendent idealism, part of which is the eternal youth's need to be loved, part of which is the generous heart's need to be used, and part of which is the mixture of altruistic foolishness and self-deception that is an ingredient of American illusion. On the professional level, Dick sacrificially had subordinated his entire career to one case. On the level of history, Dick's self-sacrifice was naively made for a world that socially and morally was not worth saving in the first place. As he wrote to Edmund Wilson, Fitzgerald knew he was creating a hero who was "an 'homme épuissé, not only an homme manqué'" (12 March 1934, *Letters,* 346).

As for confusions occasioned not by Dick but by structure, any discussion of the beginning of *Tender Is the Night* inevitably involves arguments of preference for the original or for the revised version.[18] And before the existence of a revised version, that argument, of course, was impossible for the early reviewers, whose claims that the Rosemary beginning was confusing remain an entrance to arguments for and against the revision. They are also a source of mild surprise. The 1934 edition of *Tender Is the Night* did not introduce flashbacks for the first time in literary history after all, and in any event Fitzgerald's flashback obscured nothing.[19]

The reviews of the 1930s, then, can be summed up as a very mixed response in which social issues and critical perceptions were confused with each other. Praise and disapproval were about equally mingled, and overall the book could not be said to have received a warm reception. Fitzgerald was headed into obscurity, and it is useful to remember that the Fitzgerald criticism of the decade was neither retrospective nor comprehensive. It was entirely confined to review-articles written by people who had many books to read and report on in any given week and who did not have the long perspectives of time to help them know that they were reviewing anything but a late work from a literary has-been. If there was one general observation that emerged more frequently than any other in the 1930s, it was the judgment that *Tender Is the Night* is a book of patches of brilliant, powerful, moving writing that does not come together for a sustained triumph.

THE 1940S

Although almost nothing was written about Fitzgerald in the 1940s, what criticism there was began to tug away at the shroud of obscurity that had enwrapped Fitzgerald by the time he died in the last month of 1940. As a matter of course, the early notices of the decade were obituary. Also as a matter of course, the postmortem period saw attempts at retrospective summary. Uneasily aware that perhaps Fitzgerald had been unduly neglected, the decade tried to come back to him, but the book market was too largely taken up with the hot war and then with the politics of the early cold war. The brief and scarce essays on Fitzgerald in the 1940s, most of which tried to sum up Fitzgerald, were divided in their views,[20] but the general tone was one of condescension: Scott Fitzgerald was not a perennially important writer, and *Tender Is the Night,* as John Berryman representatively said, was a slight book that will not last; it was "diffuse, lush, uncertain, and badly designed."[21] Symptomatic of the persistent element of ambivalence, however, is the fact that the same *Kenyon Review* that contained Berryman's pronouncement in the winter carried an essay in the spring in which Arthur Mizener asserted that *Tender Is the Night* is "surely Fitzgerald's most important novel for all its manifest flaws of construction."[22] The discussions of "flaws" indicate the continuing, widespread concern of all 1930s and 1940s readers with the structure of the original version: the focus on Rosemary at the beginning. For instance, Arnold Gingrich, the editor of *Esquire* and sympathetic to Fitzgerald, insisted on the problem in his obituary essay. He called *Tender Is the Night* "a magnificent failure," "the malformed twin embryo of two books, one of which might have been a masterpiece . . . [and should have been] titled simply *Richard Diver.*"[23] There is very little opening up or opening out in Fitzgerald criticism during the 1940s. Rather the opposite. One senses in the autopsy concentration on biography a closing down, a quality of quick, final, and generally disapproving summation. Judgment mistakenly identifying Fitzgerald's books and their themes with his personal life and materials in absolute terms centered on Fitzgerald as voice of and prime actor in the decadent spree of the 1920s, and on his books as essentially autobiographical celebrations of the Jazz Age. The decade persisted in critical myopia about the uses Fitzgerald made of his materials. He was, for many commentators, a marvelously evocative creator of beautifully poetic prose that never added up to anything serious for a mature world.

Nevertheless, the biographical focus of the 1940s, the desire to total him up once and for all and have done with him, did result in an underlying consciousness that there was more here than could be summed neatly in the categories that had been established in the reviews of the 1930s. And in the academy, with the conclusion of World War II, critical perspectives, especially those of the New Criticism, ushered in different ways of looking at fiction. The stirring of the countersummary is best expressed by Stephen Vincent Benet's obituary notice of Fitzgerald and the fragment of *The Last Tycoon:*

When Scott Fitzgerald died, a good many of the obituaries showed a curious note of self-righteousness. They didn't review his work, they merely reviewed the Jazz Age and said that it was closed. Because he had made a spectacular youthful success at one kind of thing, they assumed that one kind of thing was all he could ever do . . . And they were one hundred percent wrong. . . . *The Last Tycoon* shows what a really first-class writer can do with material—how he gets under the skin. . . . Wit, observation, sure craftsmanship, the verbal facility that Fitzgerald could always summon—all these . . . [and] a richness of texture, a maturity of point of view . . . [show] us what we all lost in his early death . . . the evidence is in. You can take your hats off, now, gentlemen, and I think perhaps you had better. This is not a legend, this is a reputation—and, seen in perspective, it may well be one of the most secure reputations of our time.[24]

THE 1950s

The critical reception of *Tender Is the Night* in the 1950s is marked in the very first year of the decade by the two most significant events in the development of Fitzgerald criticism and the study of *Tender Is the Night*. One is the appearance of Malcolm Cowley's edition of the revised version of the novel,[25] and the other is the publication of Arthur Mizener's *The Far Side of Paradise*.[26] The first critical biography of Fitzgerald, and still the best, Mizener's book was the first original book-length study of any kind to be published on F. Scott Fitzgerald. There had been one collection of essays by and about Fitzgerald, Edmund Wilson's edition of *The Crack-Up* in 1945 (the first book-length publication of any kind devoted entirely to Fitzgerald),[27] and it was joined in the annus mirabilis of 1951 by the first book-length collection of essays entirely about Fitzgerald, Alfred Kazin's edition of *F. Scott Fitzgerald: The Man and His Work*.[28] These books stimulated a reexamination of Fitzgerald that created a sharp increase in critical publication about him. Two years later, when Scribner's reissued *The Great Gatsby* and *Tender Is the Night* (revised version), both edited by Malcolm Cowley, and *The Last Tycoon* fragment, edited by Edmund Wilson, in *Three Novels of F. Scott Fitzgerald*, "the Fitzgerald revival" became an accomplished fact. There has been a continuous flow of work on Fitzgerald ever since.

In the early and middle 1950s the issues became less a matter of judgment about social history and more a matter of judgment about literary technique. Criticism of *Tender Is the Night* turned on arguments about the original and revised versions. And by the end of the decade investigations of Fitzgerald began to develop away from brief review-judgments and biography to analysis. Arguments about the versions continued and still continue, but analysis and interpretation remained the center of criticism in the 1960s, and by the early 1970s *Tender Is the Night* enjoyed a full and coherent body of criticism. Throughout the 1950s, although the decade finally was building a foundation for an eventual recognition of *Tender Is the Night* as a great work of American literature, criticism continued to display some of the same ambivalence that had characterized the 1930s and 1940s. There was as yet no clear consensus. Only one other book-length critical study existed in the 1950s, James E. Miller's *The Fictional Technique of Scott Fitzgerald*,[29] and Miller did not see *Tender Is the Night* or its main characters as creations of heroic identity. Periodical literature was split, the most hostile being an essay by Kingsley Amis, who, read from a distance of several decades, sounds antagonistic to the point of jealousy.[30] The (London) *Times Literary Supplement* concluded that *Tender Is the Night* was a magnificent failure (a judgment which by then had become a fashionable critical commonplace),[31] and Leslie Fiedler pronounced Fitzgerald to be an able writer about the rich, an honest writer who was capable of glowing prose but who never mastered point of view.[32] Alfred Kazin thought *Tender* a good book,[33] but John Aldridge claimed that it didn't all come together.[34] One commentator allowed *Tender Is the Night* a "slender but secure" existence as literature,[35] and one found the book to be a total bluff that could compel no one's belief.[36] Probably as representative a reading as any in the 1950s is John R. Kuehl's sympathetic essay on the book as Fitzgerald's major foray into realism.[37] The critical issues were undergoing a process of considerable change. The 1950s began to identify the major areas of fruitful investigation: Fitzgerald's relationship to his past and to its values, his moral perceptions of wealth, the novel as history, the Romantic imagination endangered by historical reality, and incest as a paradigmatic manifestation of corruption in the modern world. An essay by Richard Schoenwald adumbrated all criticism on the topic of Fitzgerald and Keats,[38] and by the time the 1960s inherited the complete legacy of the Fitzgerald revival of the 1950s, the shape, scope, topics, and pertinent issues raised by the novel were beginning to emerge amply in the critical mind.

THE 1960s AND 1970s

So copious was that critical legacy that when we arrive in the 1960s and 1970s, we find an overabundance of critical and scholarly work to be gathered by the student seeking for the first time an overview of the critical career of *Tender Is the Night*. Happily, useful scholarly and critical aids exist (consult note 12, this chapter). Two patterns in the development of the critical reception of *Tender Is the Night* in the 1960s and the 1970s deserve attention here, because they not only define the emerging shape of *Tender* in the 1980s and early 1990s, but also illustrate the profound connection between critical perceptions and the historical times. In the 1960s and early 1970s the Vietnam War divided America as had nothing since the Civil War. Those who supported the war saw nothing but good in American power; those who opposed it saw nothing but ill. Although this stark statement would require modification for any given individual or even for some of the political positions adopted, it is not a misleading indication of the intensity with which the American population was politicized into a deep and bitter division. More than any sector of American society, the university was thrown into the turmoil of the division. Fearful of the draft and sickened by the nature of the war, students and faculty generally opposed the war as an apocalyptic exposé of the realities beneath the millennialistic assumptions about America as the Redeemer Nation. The political issues should have revealed the story of Dick Diver as a parable for the times. But paradoxically, because of his Old School aura, Dick was seen by many readers as a representative rather than a victim of an imperial America. In the late 1960s, students began to find Dick Diver hard to understand and hard to take. Critics, almost all of them in the academy, began to find him retrograde. Times of deep division are not apt to be times of fine distinctions, and there grew in the literary criticism of the 1960s and 1970s—which increasingly became the voice of dissent—a perspective that held Dick to be at best a fool and at worst a villain. In the 1960s and 1970s the confusion no longer arose from uncertainties about why Dick broke down, but centered on the question of whether he deserves our sympathies. The division in Fitzgerald's fiction between the victim-hero (Dick, Gatsby), who represented the best of America, and the triumphant characters (the Buchanans, the Warrens), who represented its worst, became lost for some readers in the deep American divisions of war. As the representative American, Dick became indiscriminately identified for some as the embodiment of Romantic self-deceptions (he was that) that was the legitimization of the destructively indiscriminate uses and abuses of American power (he was not that). As one observer put it, "Over the years . . . readers have easily seen that the many more or less discrete reasons for Diver's collapse can be arranged under two broad categories. The first is socioeconomic: an idealistic, middle-class hero is used and discarded by a rich and careless leisure class. But Fitzgerald was more subtle and more honest than to confine himself to such a baldly dialectical motivation, and provided a second, psychological category of motivation by ascribing to Dick some flaw of character which made him extraordinarily susceptible to the fate which overtook him."[39]

In the 1950s, criticism had been able to take for granted the idealized concept of America as the accepted definition of goodness beset by evil actualities. But in the 1960s and 1970s the problem for criticism became more intricate, because the idealistic sense of America, acceptable as an identity for the 1950s and the 1940s, and even for the radical, restive 1930s, itself came into doubt. As essays, for instance, on the Keatsian elements in *Tender Is the Night* indicate, there is a chronologically developing sense that Romantic assumptions are inadequate, a sense of the ineluctable and inescapable morning-after of history, moving from a yearning for the realm of Dream to a nightmare vision of Dream as vampirism.[40]

Hostility to Dick also reflected anti-WASP aspects of the militant rise of consciousness and expectation in minority and women's movements and in the gay and lesbian liberation movement, as well as in neo-Marxism, in deconstructionist criticism, and in the drug culture, all of which were complex and inextricable parts of the reexamination of values occasioned by or related to the Vietnam War.[41] The changes in the nature of sexual identification, of sexual activity, of sexual acceptability, and of expectations concerning marriage and career began to make it difficult for many to understand why so much angst is associated with Dick and Rosemary's relationship. Many young readers since the 1970s think that Dick is merely stuffy and foolish and that too much is made of his gentlemanly obligations. That observation seems to argue against the enduring interest and value of *Tender Is the Night,* but what it really indicates is one more demonstration of the extent to which this book has been unlucky. Dick had to wait about 15 years to be understood in the first place. He had to wait just a shade too long, for just as criticism in the 1950s began to catch up with the dimensions and contexts of *Tender Is the Night,* the United States underwent an epochal cultural change, obscuring the contexts in which the book is best understood. The novel's own contexts of Dick's idealism and an earlier American Dream of redemption and moral obligation are clear when discerned, and they remain perennially pertinent. This is not to say that the book cannot be understood without special pleading. But this *is* to say that if the novel and the readers of the 1930s, 1940s, and 1950s shared essentially the same context, the decade of 1965–75 introduced a distance between the context of the novel and that of the reader since then. This consideration gives point to the criticism of the 1950s that outlines that context, such as Henry Dan Piper's examination of Fitzgerald's father's world.[42]

There is another current in Fitzgerald criticism in the 1960s and 1970s, one inseparable from the first and leading toward the conclusion that *Tender Is the Night* is anything but an anachronistic curio. This emerging pattern is a consensus that the novel is about history,

about the lasting interactions of power and morality, of love, temptation, and limitation, both individual and national. Increasingly, criticism of *Tender Is the Night* centers not on the facts of marriage or the
formulas of this psychological perspective or that, but on myth and
history, on the development of America as paradigmatic of Western
history. In response to the recognition that *Tender Is the Night*
requires understanding of its cultural context, for instance, one can
justly say that *Hamlet* requires similar special attention: close to the
year 2001, how much does one know about life in medieval Danish
castles or about Elizabethan assumptions about life in medieval Danish
castles? The historical comprehension is only ancillary to the emergence of worthwhile literature into its own universality and greatness.
Tender Is the Night has already begun a classic's passage down the cor-
ridor of time, just enough to require of the reader some historical
sense of its own context in order that it be appreciated most fully in its
brightly living relevance to the reader's contexts. The critical reception
of the 1960s and 1970s reveals a pattern of growing appreciation of
Tender Is the Night as a great novel about history.

THE 1980s AND 1990s

There are three major facts about the critical reception of *Tender Is the
Night* in the 1980s and early 1990s. The first is that critical essays in
the 1980s and 1990s no longer need to justify the choice of *Tender Is
the Night* as a subject worthy of serious consideration.

The second is that the great plethora of Fitzgerald criticism begins
to dwindle from profusion to dearth. In part the lessening of critical
attention to *Tender Is the Night,* which was always outdistanced by the
glut of writings on *The Great Gatsby,* is a redress of balances. It is a
movement away from an overabundance of enthusiastic critical
penances for the grudging quality of attention in the 1930s and the
silence of the 1940s. In part it is a reflection of the fact that Fitzgerald
died so young. At his death he did not leave behind a large body of
work and a developed school of acolytes and proselytizers. The wealth

of work on Fitzgerald from 1951 to 1980 created a sense that Fitzgerald's works had been exhausted by commentators and there was little left to say. Like all great literature, however, Fitzgerald's best work continues to support new insights and perspectives, and that leads us to the third aspect of the dwindling critical attention of the 1980s and early 1990s: the critical reception remains inevitably ideological. Ideology concerning race and sexual orientation have played a small part in the continuation of this critical phenomenon, but Marxism[43] and feminism[44] have played much larger parts. Fitzgerald has been praised and damned for his presentations of wealth and of women, and there has been an increased focus on Zelda.[45] Although some specialized topics like Fitzgerald and Hollywood have come to the fore as more facts about Fitzgerald are collected and organized,[46] criticism continues to center on the major thematic issues raised by Scott's books, and *Tender Is the Night* has settled into a modest but steady channel of attention that offers up four or five essays a year.[47]

OVERVIEW

No recapitulation of the critical reception of *Tender Is the Night* would be rounded out without at least a few words about books on Fitzgerald, for they indicate the intensity of response. On the quantitative level, the proliferation of Fitzgerald criticism can be seen in the fact that in the 1950s there were three books of biography or criticism devoted entirely to Fitzgerald; but even if we exclude the many books written about Fitzgerald that do not contain an extended statement about *Tender Is the Night,* and limit ourselves in the three decades from 1960 to 1990 to *only* those books with significant sections concerned with *Tender Is the Night,* we find that there were 53 books published! Seventeen were essentially concerned with biographical materials, four were collections of Fitzgerald's correspondence, seven were volumes of bibliography, and 25 were critical studies. Bruccoli's *The Composition of "Tender Is the Night"* remains the definitive study of the text.

A full checklist of criticism on *Tender Is the Night* from 1934 through 1980 can be found in Joseph Wenke's "*Tender Is the Night:* A Cross-referenced Bibliography of Criticism," in Milton R. Stern's *Critical Essays on F. Scott Fitzgerald's "Tender Is the Night."* For materials since 1980, helpful publications are Jackson Bryer's *The Critical Reputation of F. Scott Fitzgerald: Supplement One through 1981* and the annual bibliographic essays (beginning with 1963) in *American Literary Scholarship.*[48] Although the profusion of Fitzgerald criticism has diminished greatly in the 1980s and early 1990s, both the shape and the general quality of the criticism reveal clearly that Fitzgerald has taken his place among America's classic authors and that *Tender Is the Night,* in any context, has emerged and remains as one of the great books.

A READING

3

Hello, Dick Diver

"As Fitzgerald sank deeper and deeper into the bitterness of his experience, he became increasingly certain of what the rules in his own decalogue were: hard work, discipline, responsibility, courtesy, politeness, courage, rationality, order, honesty, and integrity. Fitzgerald gave these 10 commandments to Dick Diver."

Consistently over the years, as Fitzgerald discovered more and more of what his book was about, he focused on scenes in which the relationships of characters became vehicles for his delineation of the corrosion of Diver's imaginative greatness among the social types of the international postwar world. In this novel the subject matter of disease is always a metaphor, widening outward to the social heritage that it sums up rather than narrowing inward to a sensationalistic presentation of the abnormal psyche. In all 18 drafts of the novel and in his letters, it is clear that Fitzgerald is concerned with the dying fall, the long dive that becomes both the theme and the narrative method of the story. Fitzgerald arranged his scenes so that there is a constant and incremental focus on the disintegration of the diver from his initial brilliant promise to his final oblivion. The reason, in fact, that Fitzgerald worked on the eighteenth draft—the revised "final" version that he never lived to see—was that he realized that the scenes, the presentation of action, should be rearranged so that the beginning of the book is also the beginning of Dick's career, in which he is at the height of his idealistic aspirations and his almost magical powers. Fitzgerald had always planned his narrative as a dying fall. He came to feel that the merger of structure and narrative method with the enormous sense of loss he wished to dramatize demanded a straight, chronological line of Dick's dying fall, beginning at the heights and merging into events in which the diver is seen progressively sapped, losing his powers and charm, and sinking finally from sight.

The note Fitzgerald wrote to himself as he miraculously hit stride again in his work on the novel during the bitter year of 1932 is not so much an explanation of the many complex changes from draft to draft of the book as it is an explanation of what summed up the revisions as he shifted and channeled them toward the first edition: "The novel should do this," the note said: show a man who is a natural idealist, a spoiled priest, giving in for various causes to the ideas of the haute bourgeoisie, and in his rise to the top of the social world losing his idealism, his talent[,] and turning to drink and dissipation. Background one in which the leisure class is at their truly most brilliant and glamorous."[1] And as he wrote to H. L. Mencken just as the first edition was published,

> I would like to say in regard to my book that there was a deliberate intention in every part of it except the first. The first part, the romantic introduction, was too long and too elaborated largely because of the fact that it had been written over a series of years with varying plans, but everything else in the book conformed to a *definite intention* and if I had to start to write it again tomorrow I would adopt the same plan. . . . That is what most of the critics fail to understand (outside of the fact that they fail to recognize and identify anything in the book): that the motif of the "dying fall" was absolutely deliberate and did not come from any diminution of vitality but from a definite plan.[2]

The same sense of central purpose emerged four years later when Fitzgerald wrote to Maxwell Perkins about a revised version of the novel. "But I am especially concerned about *Tender*," he wrote. "Its great fault is that the *true* beginning—the young psychiatrist in Switzerland—is tucked away in the middle of the book. If pages 151–212 [the first 10 chapters of book 2] were taken from their present place and put at the start, the improvement in appeal would be enormous" (24 December 1938, *Letters*, 281).

The metaphor of the dying fall is expressed in the literal facts of war, death, loss, and departure. Dick Diver's decalogue, his lost "beautiful lovely safe world[,] blew itself up with a great gust of high explosive love" (57) born of the accumulated identities and certainties of the generations of the long past. The certainties, which turned out to be betrayals, resulted in the illusions cataclysmically destroyed in the Great War. The dead of World War I, mourned by Dick during his visit with Abe and Rosemary to the trenches below Thiepval (56–59), are in effect buried in the same graveyard with all of Dick's forefathers in the family cemetery. The dying fall makes *Tender Is the Night* a series of goodbyes to lost hopes. The novel is saturated with events and signs of departure and the end of things.

Dick Diver is a "spoiled priest" in two senses: he is cosseted and idolized by his admirers; he is also a devotee in the highest vocation of redemptive healing, unequal, as any mortal would be, to the absolute, millennial quality of his calling. As spoiled priest, Dick is intricately and inextricably associated with both the dream America and the actual America. Like Fitzgerald in the two worlds of his art and his actual life, not only is the drunk ruined by wealth and power, but so also is the potential world-redeemer self-ruined by his own charm, by his illusion-filled responses to his own deepest need to be liked and loved. As a composite fictive character, Dick is his creator and his creator's nation. "I am part of the race consciousness," Fitzgerald once told his secretary. "I take people to me and change my conception of them and then write them out again. My characters are all Scott Fitzgerald,"[3] fully as much as the characters that Dick took to him and, as he said, "worked over" were all Diver creations of the composite moment. Fitzgerald restored people to an essential meaning as he remade them into part of a character, just as Dick restored people to an essential identity in his creative moments: "It was themselves he gave back to them, blurred by the compromises of how many years" (52). Because they were made whole by the love-need of the American doctor's eager and self-sacrificial leap to service, the people around Dick must reflect the goodness he dreams, must be good, if only for the moment of the perfect dinner in the perfect garden in the perfect evening in the moon goddess dream world of the Villa Diana. Ever the healing psychiatrist, Dick realizes that he himself was in part a composite of all the personalities he had loved, and "for the remainder of his life . . . was condemned to carry with him the egos of certain people, early met and early loved, and to be only as complete as they were complete themselves" (245). In his purpose and his aspirations, the healer was the redeemer. But no mere mortal could be anything but overwhelmed by treating the actual world in the context of the transcendent one. "Diver" consequently has a double meaning. It names the would-be redeemer who dives deep beneath appearances into realities, and it names the man who, in the process, takes the long dive of the dying fall.

Symbolically, Dick carries on his shoulders his transcendent aspirations, his love, and the sins of the world, as they are summed up in Nicole. The cross he picks up is her "case." Dick is at once a glorious Romantic fool and a tragic Romantic hero. Fitzgerald's hero is more than a spoiled priest; he is a failed Christ. Even in the pathetic depths of his Romantic failure, he knew that "we must all try to be good" (185).

4

Categories of Identity

What was good was what was demanded by the moral decalogue of the old virtues and graces. For Dick Diver, as for Scott Fitzgerald, the true—the *good*—romantic[1] (to shift to Fitzgerald's own lowercase use of the term) was one who felt the delighted exhilaration of wonder and unlimited expectation, who vibrated with exciting intimations of transcendent possibility and identity. But Fitzgerald confronted his own self-recognition that the romantic personality also could be the bad romantic, could merely wallow irresponsibly in the impulse of the enchanted evening and in the ugly depression of the morning after. The romantic was energized by illusions and imagination, but was also destroyed by them. What Fitzgerald characterized as "Irish" and "female" within himself (as within Dick Diver and Rosemary Hoyt) was the romantic. For him the ideal of Keatsian Romanticism had to triumph in art, as the romantic decidedly did not in life. Therefore, the "good"—rational responsibility, integrity, hard work, the old virtues and graces that activated the romantic's imagination into art—was the mark of maturity.

If the true artist is mature in his self-consuming dedication and responsibility, the world of actuality in its irresponsibility remains, morally speaking, in "Baby" Warren diapers, on what Dick knows is "the nursery footing" (84) of teenage Rosemary's crush on him. In Fitzgerald's fiction there is an intense and focused concentration on rational responsibility defined as goodness and maturity—the honesty, courage, and discipline to accept and clean up after the consequences of one's own actions. Carraway had that virtue and grace in *The Great Gatsby* as the Buchanans and their whole world did not; Diver had that virtue and grace in *Tender Is the Night* as the Warrens and their whole world did not. The ability to assume burdens required the old virtues articulated consciously: the agendas of rational order such as Dick redemptively imposes on the chaos of Nicole's life. For Fitzgerald only by the imposition of rational order is the romantic healingly creative and able rather than impulsively destructive.

Fitzgerald's notebooks indicate that he intended the name Diver to suggest a romantic who fell from a great height of shining promise. Fitzgerald was aware of the complex significances he was putting into the loss of the dream in *Tender Is the Night*. "'If you liked *The Great Gatsby*,' he inscribed a book for a friend, 'for God's sake read this. *Gatsby* was a tour de force, but this is a confession of faith.' Into *Tender Is the Night* he put his hard-earned beliefs: that work was the only dignity; that it didn't help a serious man to be too much flattered and loved; that money and beauty were treacherous aides; that honor, courtesy, courage—the old fashioned virtues—were the best guides after all" (Turnbull 1962, 241). Insofar as the novel was a metaphoric history of himself, the writing of *Tender Is the Night* was not only an act of contrition for Fitzgerald, but also an act of redemption. It was, like all his deepest immersions in his art, expurgation and salvation.

In this context one could say that in addition to all the other things it is, *Tender Is the Night* is also a morality play about the nature of charm. True charm, such as that exercised by Dick before his internal self began to disintegrate, is that of the hard, disciplined "Irish," "female" romantic, responsibly and altruistically tender to people even in little things. True charm is the creative imagination that wishes to heal and to make others feel and be good. True charm is sensitively putting oneself constructively at the service of other people's psychic needs. But false charm is merely a manner, a stale reflex left over after the high morale of inner moral purpose has been destroyed. The disintegrating Dick Diver recognizes that "the manner lasts long after the morale has cracked." Toward the conclusion of the novel, the bitter, rising hilarity hidden within Dick Diver, as he comes to realize what an absurd fool he has been, wastefully sacrificing his talents in the service of what he sees too late as a decadent world not worth saving, is the sign of his weary self-mockery and his disgust with the world he has inhabited. Dick's revulsion with himself and with the world is the final honesty reserved for him, the ruthless self-awareness that Fitzgerald insisted was the sine qua non for every artist. As he always did, Fitzgerald used the meanings of his own life for the creation of his fiction. Whether we see *Tender Is the Night* as a morality play about charm, a historical novel about the decline of the West, a moral history of America, a psychological novel of inner disintegration, or a tragicomic novel of manners, the dying fall of Dr. Richard Diver is the uniting center of all the book's topics, motifs, and themes.

Dr. Diver, in the process of his most successful and most bitter cure—his deliberate transference of Nicole from himself to Tommy Barban as the completion of her new health—creates his greatest Christly act of final, self-sacrificial service as a medical practitioner and his most painfully loving act of the good romantic charm. But by that time his continued expenditure of self at the service of the world about him has reduced him to internal ruin, and all that he has left is a horrified realization of how he has mistakenly wasted his promise in a lavish expenditure that has only turned out to be pandering rather than redemption. He never knew it along most of the way. He gave himself in good faith and in all illusion. One can only say of Dick what Owl Eyes said of Gatsby: "The poor son of a bitch." All that he's left with is an internal nothingness in which all love and friendships are either dead or empty jokes.

Unaware that he was near the end of his life, Fitzgerald wrote to his longtime friend and editor, Maxwell Perkins, "Once I believed in friendship, believed I *could* (if I didn't always) make people happy and it was more fun than anything. Now even that seems like a vaudevillian's cheap dream of heaven, a vast minstrel show in which one is the perpetual Bones" (20 May 1940, *Letters,* 288). So Dick Diver, in the unceasing, self-aware honesty about what has been happening to him, says with slow sadness, "I guess I'm the Black Death. . . . I don't seem to bring people happiness any more" (219). And Abe North, in his heavy despair at the failure of his life in his destructive and impulsive alcoholic charm, says, "Tired of friends. The thing is to have syco-phants" (81). The "trick of the heart," as Dick calls it, of friendship and happiness is distinct from the trick of manners, just as the good and bad charm and the good and bad romantic are distinct from each other.

Distinct in the same way is the difference between true and false femaleness and maleness in the novel. In *Tender Is the Night* the war-fare between the sexes and the breakdown of sexual identities, like the warfare among nations and the breakdown of national identities are a dimension of the exploded old decalogues in the "broken universe of the war's ending" (245).

5

Sexual Identities and Baby Identities

Categorized within the framework of his motif of sexual identities in *Tender Is the Night,* F. Scott Fitzgerald, with some justification, could be labeled a sexist and a homophobe. As the previous pages have indicated, Fitzgerald's insistence on the old virtues and graces reveal the extent to which there was an essentially conservative core at the center of his values. The politically liberal Fitzgerald was philosophically conservative to the extent that he sought not revolution but the identification and retention of what he saw as the essence of goodness in the mixed past. But ideological issues are complicated, and the seductive ease with which we might label the early twentieth-century Fitzgerald by the narrow application of late twentieth-century ideological contexts is by its very nature a dangerous ease through which the intricate artistic complexity and current applicability of his work can be oversimplified and lost.

By American standards at the close of the twentieth century, Fitzgerald was sexist to the extent that he saw the world, in his early twentieth-century context, as one in which the male leads and the female follows. But whatever the predispositions with which one comes to *Tender Is the Night,* it is necessary to trace the motif of sexual identities within the context in which Fitzgerald worked in order to glimpse the intricacy and antisexist intentions of that motif. For Fitzgerald the context was one in which the givens were that women had been oppressively subordinated to men and that now, finally, the "emergent Amazons" were breaking out; but the world into which they were breaking out was nothing but a moral chaos in which there were really no functions, identities, or values except social transmogrifications of the wrongs that had always existed. Women taking power, consequently, did not become fulfilled people; rather, they merely became female "men." In the ideal suppositions of the lost world of virtues and graces, men, on the other hand, in their dependability as leaders, had had to bear full responsibility and provide complete reliability for the possibilities they afforded for their women as individual human beings. In the postwar world, however, the women had begun to assume independent power, based, ironically, either on their desirability as sex objects (Rosemary Hoyt, Nicole) or on their independent "male" control of money (Baby Warren). Men, emerging into the same world of fixed identities dissolving in an unfixed world of moral anarchy, could assume domination only in a blind insistence on the old fixed sexual identities. But for Fitzgerald such insistence reduced maleness to essentially mindless, mere brute power (Tommy Barban). Or men abandoned their basic sexual responsibilities and reliabilities (Devereux Warren) and became irresponsible dependents (Abe North), fulfilling what formerly had been, supposedly, the prerogatives of the fickle "weaker sex." As women merely became female "men," men merely became male "women," and in weaving this intricacy Fitzgerald uses homosexuality as a metaphor for confused sexual identity. Consequently, within the historical context of *Tender Is the Night* homosexuality and transsexuality are identified with the heritage of the corrupt fathers as the epitome of the confusion of sexual identities that emerges in the postwar world.

As "Daddy's Girl" becomes the sexual adult that Collis Clay identifies as "Mama's girl," Rosemary becomes "economically . . . a boy, not a girl" (40). So too, daddy's boy can become daddy's girl: the Chilean counterpart of Devereux Warren, associated with him even in the similarity of their hotel apartments, is Señor Pardo y Ciudad Real.

"Warren was a strikingly handsome man . . . tall, broad, well made . . . and he had that special air about him of having known the best of this world" (125). Señor Real was a "handsome, iron-gray Spaniard, noble of carriage, with all the appurtenances of wealth and power" (243). As Warren with his male incest had made his child, so Pardo y Ciudad Real with his male, authoritarian bullyings and whippings had intensified his. His boy has become a "girl," the "Queen of Chile" (244). Warren left it to the doctors to clean up the mess of a daddy's girl he had made. Real too calls in the doctors to clean up the mess of a daddy's "girl" he has made. Ironically, in the world of anarchic identities (the novel associates the idea of anarchy with the dissolution of identities in the new postwar world), women continue to be victims and casualties in the process of emergence (the eczema patient in Dick's clinic) as grievously as they were (Nicole Warren) in the pre-emergent world of fixed identities that had always concealed destructive behavior in the first place. In sum, although Fitzgerald, as a product of his time and place, was trapped within homophobic and sexist stereotypes, he uses those very stereotypes to create a breathtakingly multifarious antisexist motif. In some very nonconservative ways this essentially conservative writer saw what the issues were, and he expressed them in artistically gorgeous patterns that transcend the received ideologies of particular time and place.

Whether his materials demanded male or female characters, Fitzgerald felt that the postwar world he was writing about was really a woman's world. Adapting to the new world, the golden girl finds *irresponsible* power in her liberation from the man's world of old. The emergent Amazon ends up as the female personification of her hot tom, and she succeeds in the war for control. Ironically, therefore, her triumph signals no moral liberation but merely a transference of "maleness," a triumph of continuing selfishness, vanity, impulse, and irresponsible dominion over the old virtues and graces. In *Tender Is the Night* the breakdown of sexual identities is a sign of the breakdown of moral identities, one with metaphors of war and combat as signs of the breakdown of a civilization.

Fitzgerald chronicled in the sordid history of the Warren clan the extent to which men betrayed their old ideal role. He saw that the day when women merely followed was over and that the limited identity of handmaiden would no longer suffice. He saw that in the warfare between men and women, victory in the brave new world was, tragically, not personality and freedom but merely power and money increasingly at the service of "female" whim. He saw the consumerist spree of the Roaring Twenties as a feminized version of the essence of capitalism. He saw in irresponsible "female" exertions of "male" checkbook strength the continuing exploitation of the world's creative labors and the corrupting misuse of imaginative romantic aspiration. Wastefully extravagant excesses of human wealth, to which the political sexuality of money lends great *charm,* are made explicit in the famous class-conscious passage describing Nicole's sybaritic shopping raids:

> Nicole bought from a great list that ran two pages, and bought the things in the windows besides. Everything she liked that she couldn't possibly use herself, she bought as a present for a friend. She bought colored beads, folding beach cushions, artificial flowers, honey, a guest bed, bags, scarfs, love birds, miniatures for a doll's house, and three yards of some new cloth the color of prawns. She bought a dozen bathing suits, a rubber alligator, a travelling chess set of gold and ivory, big linen handkerchiefs for Abe, two chamois leather jackets of king-fisher blue and burning bush from Hermes—bought all these things not a bit like a high-class courtesan buying underwear and jewels, which were after all professional equipment and insurance, but with an entirely different point of view. Nicole was the product of much ingenuity and toil. For her sake trains began their run at Chicago and traversed the round belly of the continent to California; chicle factories fumed and link belts grew link by link in factories; men mixed toothpaste in vats and drew mouthwash out of copper hogsheads; girls canned tomatoes quickly in August or worked rudely at the Five-and-Tens on Christmas Eve; half-breed Indians toiled on Brazilian coffee plantations and dreamers were muscled out of patent rights in new tractors—these were some of the people who gave a tithe to Nicole and, as the whole system swayed and thundered onward, it lent a feverish bloom to such processes of hers as wholesale buying, like the flush of a fireman's face holding his

post before a spreading blaze. She illustrated very simple princi-
ples, containing in herself her own doom, but illustrated them so
accurately that there was grace in the procedure, and presently
Rosemary would try to imitate it. (54–55)

In the implicitly Marxist view in which Fitzgerald sees Nicole's
"women's" activity, the Daddy's Girl created by Devereux Warren
becomes the paradigm for what Rosemary, the nation's Daddy's Girl,
will harden into. Nicole is the perfected product of capitalist opulence.
She is the desirable gorgeousness Abe had yearned for—"he had been
heavy, belly-frightened, with love for her for years" (81). When, in the
golden girl's gorgeous world, Abe has become a shambling wreck of
himself through destructive alcoholic self-indulgence, "he spoke up
suddenly" and made a peculiar statement. "Tired of women's worlds,"
he said (81). In the destructive users in *Tender Is the Night* Fitzgerald
brought to fullest and richest fruition what was adumbrated in the friv-
olous debs and popular daughters of *This Side of Paradise,* the golden
bitch of *The Beautiful and Damned,* the rich boys and girls and winter
dreams of the short stories, and Daisy and Jordan of *The Great
Gatsby.*

Among the white-fleshed (5) newcomers to the beach—syco-
phants like Mrs. Abrams, arrivists like the McKiscos, pale, colorless
bores all—are Dumphrey and Campion, two homosexuals. Fitzgerald
presents Dumphrey and Campion comically to signal the serious
breakdown of identity that invades the painstakingly constructed
world Dick had built. When, for a sexual joke, Dick wears the swim
trunks Nicole had made for him, a garment that looks like "black lace
drawers" (but "close inspection revealed that actually they were lined
with flesh-colored cloth"), McKisco's reaction is merely funny: "'Well,
if that isn't a pansy's trick!' exclaimed Mr. McKisco contemptuously—
then turning quickly to Mr. Dumphrey and Mr. Campion he added,
'Oh, I beg your pardon'" (21). On the other hand, pronouncedly sexist
macho identity is also reduced to a bad joke. Tommy Barban's domi-
neering maleness, typified by the hard, fixed convention of the code
duello, is reduced to pretentious silliness by McKisco's unfamiliarity
with its ways and by Campion's gasping, squealing voyeurism.

Significantly, when the macho male can take no more of the civilization he lives in, he too wants to get away from women. "This fight's
between two men," Abe explains to Rosemary, referring to the duel,
and adds, "—what Tommy needs is a good war" (44).

In his final proprietorship of the desirable golden girl, as in all his
characteristics, macho Tom Barban displays the qualities that marked
The Great Gatsby's macho Tom Buchanan: the same arrogance, the
same brute physical power, the same boredom coupled with the same
inability to bear ennui, the same moral pointlessness of his drift
through life coupled with the same unprofitable fretfulness of a life
without imaginative goals, the same condescension, the same nostalgia
for combat activity. "He was tall and his body was hard but overspare,
save for the bunched force gathered in his shoulders and upper arms . . .
there was a faint disgust always in his face which marred the full fierce
lustre of his brown eyes. Yet one remembered them afterward, when
one had forgotten the inability of the mouth to endure boredom and
the young forehead with its furrows of fretful and unprofitable pain"
(18). Except in his desire for women, this hot tom is essentially insen-
sitive to people, especially to other men. "He did not like any man
very much or feel men's presence with much intensity—he was all
relaxed for combat" (197). "Tommy Barban was a ruler, Tommy was
a hero" (196), and Fitzgerald fits him to the historical circumstances of
the emergent Amazon's world. Even Tommy's laugh is a "martial
laugh: 'Um-buh—ha-ha! Um-buh—ha-ha!'" (196). His values are those
only of self-interest and physical immediacy. He doesn't care what he
fights for. As Tommy recounts his rescue of the ancient, desiccated
Russian prince, during which he and the prince killed three red guards,
"Dick decided that this parched papier-mâché relic of the past was
scarcely worth the lives of three young men" (198). But Barban has a
simple sense of history and allegiances. His resistance to change is not
part of the Old World graces and virtues, but the simplest proprietary
reaction that is military cousin to the heavy, careful selfishness of bourgeois Franz: "'Well, I'm a soldier,' Barban . . . [says] pleasantly. 'My
business is to kill people. I fought against the Riff because I'm a
European, and I fought the Communists because they want to take my
property from me'" (35). He is suited to the emergent Amazons,

knowing all the "old Languedoc peasant remedies" (295) for subduing and living with their combative independence. Devoid of fine sensibilities compared with Abe and Dick, Barban is "less civilized, more skeptical and scoffing, his manners were formal, even perfunctory" (19). He is sophisticated in the techniques of survival and victory, both military and sexual. That earnest cipher, McKisco, has no idea, when he argues war and politics with Tommy, of "what he was up against with Barban, neither of the simplicity of the other man's bag of ideas nor of the complexity of his training" (35). Tommy is Fitzgerald's prototype for the aura of fascism and the fascist warrior.

The man of Languedoc remedies is a constant in Fitzgerald's fiction. He is prefigured in the beefy diamond-in-the-rough football hero, Langueduc, in *This Side of Paradise*. In *The Beautiful and Damned* there is the successful moviemaker, blocky Bloeckman, who knocks down the protagonist, Anthony, and who is powerful and a successful womanizer in the male business world Anthony cannot crack. None of the avatars of the type has moonlit dreams, none has any of what Fitzgerald referred to variously as "female," "Irish," and "romantic" sensibility; none has any sympathy for such imagination. Barban and Dick dislike each other. As the hard simplification of values allowed by barbarism, Tommy is the enemy of the complex, polite, and imaginative civilization that reached its creative apogee in the virtues and graces of Richard Diver. As Rosemary sums up the men she meets, she sees that "Barban was less civilized" and that "Abe North had, under his shyness, a desperate humor that amused but puzzled her. . . . But Dick Diver—he was all complete. . . . His voice, with some faint Irish melody running through it, wooed the world, yet she felt the layer of hardness in him, of self-control and of self-discipline, her own virtues" (19).

For Barban Dick's sensitive, controlled energy in the service of women—a responsible and civilized morality that Tommy calls "this 'kind' bullying"—is emasculating and suffocating. He has no sense of the strength and disciplined self-sacrifice it takes for Dick to "build out some broken side till it was better than the original structure" (116). When Dick thinks that phrase, at the optimistic beginning of his youthful aspirations, he is referring to his own need for creatively destructive experience. Aware of himself as the lucky, as yet unspoiled

Edenic American, he significantly makes an oblique reference to Adam's rib. The true male is the *good* daddy who nurtures the female that is inextricably part of himself. As the punning thrust of his name suggests, Dr. Dick is the curative good male; but Barban, impatient with "female" delicacies and complications, cannot understand Dick's transcendent aim and heroic struggle as the man of cures. "When I'm in a rut," he tells Rosemary, "I come to see the Divers, because then I know that in a few weeks I'll want to go to war" (30). In his own rutting needs for physical action and simplifying violence, Barban is the self-indulgent tom who is merely the male mirror image of the lavishly seductive new Daddy's Girl. Savage homophobia arises not from the comic homophobia with which Fitzgerald used the values of his time and place to express wider moral ideas, but from the totalitarian machismo of the Barban character that Fitzgerald repudiated. Ironically, the merely self-gratifying unmistakable male and female confusingly become each other; their moral identities are indistinguishable one from the other.

Fitzgerald's true sexist, Tommy, wants in the female only the most basic gratification of his own hard male impulse. Dick wants in the female a rich, full human identity. Quite aware of the implications of language, Fitzgerald puns with Dr. Diver's idealistic aspirations when he has Dick, amusedly musing on his promising future as a man, whisper to himself, "Lucky Dick, you big stiff" (116). In contrast, martial Tommy's erect male hardness aspires only to "all the old Languedoc peasant" plowings (295). That macho limitation makes sexual identities clear and simple, but it robs them of all the dimensions Dick tried to create in *his* careful doctoring.

What the toms and golden girls of the new world want is not what Dick represents, but freedom from the old virtues and graces, and in that freedom they find a liberated identity. As representatives of economic dominance they want their pleasures now, however they can get them. And in fact the money heritage of the new world made by their daddies is a history of their desires. Sid Warren, the granddaddy founder of the family's legendary Chicago fortune and ducal standing, began as a midwestern meat thief: he was a horse-trading crook. His "white eyes" are the sign of his legacy. When Tommy Barban and the new, money-bright, cured Nicole run off for pure sexual release and impulsive self-gratification, Tommy asks her, "When did you begin to have white crook's eyes?" Nicole's reply is exquisitely apt. "'I have no mirror here,' she said, . . . 'but if my eyes have changed it's because I'm well again. And being well perhaps I've gone back to my true self—I suppose my grandfather was a crook and I'm a crook by heritage, so there we are'" (292). Their conversation is apposite in every way:

> "All this taming of women!" he scoffed.
> "In any society there are certain—" She felt Dick's ghost prompting at her elbow but she subsided at Tommy's overtone:
> "I've brutalized many men into shape, but I wouldn't take a chance on half the number of women. Especially this 'kind' bullying—what good does it do anybody?—you or him or anybody?'
> Her heart leaped up and then sank faintly with a sense of what she owed Dick." (293)

Cured, Nicole is free to re-enter the world of impulsive self-gratification, but now in a position of control. She is no longer the dependent child at the mercy of the daddy male. She is able to take her place in the sun world of toms because her male wealth allows her to enact the force of the independent adulthood that has been Dick's ultimate gift to her. "Nicole had been designed for change, for flight, with money as fins and wings" (280). The sexuality of wealth that Gatsby recognized in Daisy's seductive voice—"'Her voice is full of money,' he said suddenly"—is what Tommy knows is true of Nicole. She is too rich, and therefore too free, to be bound in her liberated brave new world to the kindly, bullying discipline of Dick's old virtues and graces that make sanity out of madness and clean order out of moral garbage. She protests only weakly to Tommy as she thinks of what she owes to Dick:

> "I suppose I've got—"
> "You've got too much money," he said impatiently. "That's the crux of the matter. Dick can't beat that." (293)

Indeed he can't. He becomes bankrupt, having spent all his young, American force in the illusion of what he was redeeming. Dick can no longer be the inseminating male force, the fruitful, creative female romantic, the omnisexual combination of civilized goodness that changes raw male and female into the fullest identities of man and woman. Lucky Dick is no longer the big stiff. Formerly a strong swimmer, as he tries to show off on the aquaplane for Rosemary, the diver *épuissé* discovers he no longer has the male strength and power to get up. Literally, metaphorically, and symbolically he goes limp in the water, totally spent by the cumulative self-destructive sacrifice with which he gives Nicole her freedom in her Warren world. There, the golden-girl female restored, she is the fitting complement to her mating Tom. "It's very hard taking care of white eyes—especially the ones made in Chicago," she says to him. But this hard doctor does not reply with the civilized virtues and graces of Dr. Diver: "I know all the old Languedoc peasant remedies," says Tom.

Nicole, naked, primitive, and unrestricted female now, is free at last to enjoy the sexual passion her father had robbed from her, that Dick had painstakingly fully restored to her, and that Tommy represents in the most elemental form. Fitzgerald knew exactly what he was doing when he had the newly free Nicole turn to Tommy and experience her freedom as an impulse of the moment. With her new tom beside her in the car, she

> drew in her breath, hunched her shoulders with a wriggle, and turned to Tommy.
> "Have we *got* to go all the way to your hotel in Monte Carlo?" (294)

Free as any male, now, in her self-gratifying sexual identity, Nicole is associated at once with the irresponsibility that is the privilege of the Warren wealth. "Tommy's assertion" that Nicole has white crook's eyes "seemed to absolve her from all blame or responsibility and she had a thrill of delight in thinking of herself in a new way. New vistas appeared ahead, peopled with the faces of many men, none of whom she need obey or even love" (294). And then, mindlessly heedless in her free act of passion, "struggling a little still, like a decapitated animal she forgot about Dick and her new white eyes, forgot Tommy himself and sank deeper and deeper into the minute and the moment" (294).

For Fitzgerald the bitter, hilarious irony is that free at last from the virtues and graces of responsibility, the emergent new female, in her enactment of freedom as sex, dramatizes the old female role of sex object. In the new barbarian oversimplification of the sexes, when Amazons and martial heroes merge, identity is merely a clash of desires in which the male rides the female: Barban literally is in the saddle when "symbolically . . . [Nicole] lay across . . . [Tom's] saddle-bow as surely as if he had wolfed her away from Damascus and they had come out upon the Mongolian plain" (297–98). He subdues her with his peasant remedies (suggested in the wordplay on variations of *Languedoc,* from "tongue doc" to "long dick") that provide the only relationship with women he thinks worthwhile or necessary. In the depths of her new moment, the emergent Amazon ironically surrenders all the armor Dick had fashioned for her as a controlling defense against the anarchic moment that had led to bloody sheets and madness. Goodbye to all Dick's heritage and hello anew to the anarchic Warren legacy. "Moment by moment all that Dick had taught her fell away and she was ever nearer to what she had been in the beginning, prototype of that obscure yielding up of swords that was going on in the world about her. Tangled with love in the moonlight she welcomed the anarchy of her lover" (298).

Nicole's story is the summation of Fitzgerald's continuing tale of the emergent golden girl. As such, in its various dimensions it subsumes within itself aspects of Rosemary Hoyt, Baby Warren, Mary North Minghetti, Lady Caroline Sibley-Biers, and implicitly thereby, a generation of identity formation and dissolution. At the beginning the young, raped Nicole suppresses an impulse to be a Warren who simply gets what she wants. Wanting Dick overpoweringly, "for a moment she entertained a desperate idea of telling him how rich she was, what big houses she lived in, that really she was a valuable property—for a moment she made herself into her grandfather, Sid Warren, the horse-trader. But she survived the temptation to confuse all values" (143).

But ironically, as she grows stronger she becomes destructive of Dick's willingness of the heart that had given her sustenance and support, and, fittingly, she ends up continuing the history of the Warrens. She is one of Fitzgerald's versions of the history of the allure of America. In her youth the new America appears to be the gorgeous moment to the world. Nicole has everything associated with golden promise: freshness, vigor, beauty, wealth, power. Fitzgerald's imagery makes the emergent young American golden girl the distillation of the center of the Western world. In Europe her colors are those of the blue lake and sky, the white tennis courts and clouds of "the heartless beauty" of "the true center of the western world" (147). When Dick meets her on the Swiss funicular, the world of that colorful summer morning is one of brilliant, sparkling blue and pink and gold and white. Fluffy golden clouds in the powder blue sky float above the rich, trailing roses that flick into the funicular windows as the car ascends in that rich and sun-drenched color-bright world. When Nicole bursts into that scene, Fitzgerald gives her light golden "fine-spun hair . . . fluffed into curls," and in her "sweater of powder blue and a white tennis skirt she was the first morning in May" (148). Her hair is "new," she "floats" as she sways in the funicular "between the blues of two heavens," and she rises to the fresher air of a higher world as the descending car, which takes on the burden of weight in its descent, pulls her up her rose-bestrewn way. She emerges into a new heaven as Dick, who is to take on her burden, will dive through a long dying fall in a relationship that makes the funicular ride a symbol of the central plot. As she emerges in the happy newness of the golden world she had been locked out of, she begins almost at once, within her diffident newness, to assert her Warren eyes with tennis skirt to match. She accuses Dick of not giving her a chance to make him fall in love with her, to which Dick replies,

> "*What!*"
> "The impertinence, the right to invade implied, astounded him. Short of anarchy [exactly what Nicole would come to welcome in sex with Tommy Barban] he could not think of any chance that Nicole Warren deserved." (154)

She will heal within Dick's protection against the carelessness of the sun-hot new world, "under a roof of umbrellas" on the sun-scarred beach (6); always, until she uses Dick up, "her beauty, tentatively nesting and posing, flowed into his love, ever braced to protect it" (176). But in Dick's protective domain she does not fully come out into the harsh new sunlight. Inevitably, she becomes restive as she becomes stronger in the delicately calibrated emergence Dick has planned, for she has nothing but the self Dick gives her as he brings her along toward that moment when she will have her own fully healed and healthily independent self-hood. Along the way, when Dick is gone she is nothing, has nothing, both requiring and resenting her dependence:

> She led a lonely life owning Dick, who did not want to be owned.
> Many times he had tried unsuccessfully to let go his hold on her. They had many fine times together, fine talks between the loves of the white nights, but when he turned away from her into himself he left her holding Nothing in her hands and staring at it, calling it many names, but knowing that it was only the hope that he would come back soon. (180)

Ironically, because the old virtues and graces are dead in the hot new world of broken decalogues, the only identity available to the Warren girl is the Warren identity that had despoiled her. Her hardening into health is her hardening into joyful adaptation to the decadent world from which Dick had saved her by giving her himself.

In marrying Dick Nicole had made the first necessary transference—had married a daddy she knew she could trust. Then she is able to entertain the child's subconscious wish for the death of the parent. Like the child who wants both protection and freedom, Nicole loves and hugs Dick at the same time that she wishes to cast him off so that she can be free of the restrictive decencies he imposes on her. In her mad scene at the fair, Nicole, having almost killed Dick, the children, and herself, and having wrecked the car, laughs

> hilariously, unashamed, unafraid, unconcerned. . . .
> "You were scared, weren't you?" she accused him. "You wanted to live!" (192).

As she takes on her Warren identity, "Dicole" dissolves into Nicole and a used-up Dick. The ruin of Dick is the ruin of *his* Nicole in the re-creation of the real Nicole. Having used him to extinction with the burden of herself, in one gripping moment of remorse, regret, grief, love, and pity Nicole recognizes her debt to him, even unto death. On Golding's *Margin* Dick says to her, "You ruined me, did you. . . . Then we're both ruined" (273), as for an instant he is about to dive off the yacht into a suicide that is all that's left to him; as he pauses, Nicole puts her hands in his in an invitation to take her with him. It was far from Fitzgerald's purpose to create in Nicole a one-dimensional villainess. He succeeded in creating a complex and sympathetic character the reader could both understand and pity. But the main direction of Fitzgerald's purpose in the development of her character, in which he also succeeded, is the depiction of an awakening and then triumphant Warrenism. Her first reaction to the consciously expressed thought of complete independence is fear and disbelief. Tommy tells her that she shouldn't let Dick drink. "'I!' she exclaimed in amazement. '*I* tell Dick what he should or shouldn't do!'" (274). But it isn't long before the seed planted by Tommy sprouts. Considering the possibility of Tommy, Nicole "was somewhat shocked at the idea of being interested in another man—but other women have lovers—why not me? . . . Why shouldn't I?" (276).

In her garden, as Nicole, unseen, contemplates sexual independence, the background for her thoughts is a conversation between two gardeners—"I laid her down there"—in which the sexual conflict is reawakened as she overhears the male world, with all the inhibitions and fears it gives her in memories of the brute sexuality of her father. But she can cope with it now. Trusting Dick completely in her use of him, she has no doubts about what will happen when Dick has completed her—which is when she will be finished with Dick. She yearns for the life afterward, without him; all she fears is the moment of the break itself, when she first will stand free of him. "For what might occur thereafter she had no anxiety—she suspected that that would be the lifting of a burden, an unblinding of eyes. . . . Nicole could feel the fresh breeze already—it was the wrench she feared, and the dark manner of its coming" (280). When it's Dick that's down, sinking beneath the burden of her ascent, unable any longer to lift a burden and aquaplane with it, there will be no reversal of roles. Watching Diver's humiliating defeat in the water, Nicole found that "her panic changed suddenly to contempt. . . . Nicole was annoyed—everything he did annoyed her now" (285). The impatience of the child who is grown enough to be unable to wait to be through with daddy is what is necessary for the breakthrough into one's own life. And like the child, Nicole cannot stop to consider what happens to the good daddy who gave her life.

A fine psychiatrist, Dick knew the role he played in Nicole's life, and he prepared Tommy Barban as one of the sun-world males the golden girl would leap to when she divorced him: "Tommy is one of those men that Dick passed along to Nicole" (43). In the passing Nicole will break out of her orbit around Dick's protective warmth and will pass from Dick's carefully modulated sunshine to the white glare of the garish thing that the Warren-Barban world has made of what was once Dick's beach. Everything of Dick is obliterated as a result of the ironic success of his altruism. "Since the evening on Golding's yacht," Nicole had known "a renewal of her apprehension that Dick was contriving at some desperate solution" (279). She "had a sense of being cured in a new way. Her ego began blooming like a great rich rose ['*Defense de cueillir les fleurs*,' the funicular signs had warned Dick] as she scrambled back along the labyrinths in which she had wandered for years. She hated the beach, resented the places where she had played planet to Dick's sun" (289). She "was afraid of what was in Dick's mind; again she felt that a plan underlay his current actions and she was afraid of his plans," and yet she knew that *this* good and all-wise daddy planned for her what she needed. "That he no longer controlled her—did he know that? Had he willed it all?" Condescendingly feeling "sorry for Dick as she had sometimes felt for Abe North and his ignoble destiny, sorry as for the helplessness of infants and the old," she dimly suspected that Dick had deliberately brought about her freedom from him. "'Why, I'm almost complete,' she thought. 'I'm practically standing alone without him.' And like a happy child, wanting the completion as soon as possible, and knowing vaguely that Dick had planned for her to have it, she lay on her bed as soon as she got home and wrote Tommy Barban in Nice a short provocative letter" (289). All Baby will say is, "That's what you were educated for, Doc." Nicole, in a modification of the statement, at least says, "Thanks." But when she's "all new *like a baby*," she's new "with white eyes" (295, italics added). So, "with the opportunistic memory of women she scarcely recalled how she had felt when she and Dick had possessed each other in secret places around the corners of the world, during the month before they were married. Just so had she lied to Tommy last night, swearing to him that never before had she been so entirely, so completely, so utterly" (300). And so, entirely, completely, and utterly Fitzgerald carried through this part of his "General Plan" for the novel, a part that reads, "The Divers, *as a marriage,* are at the end of their resources. Medically Nicole is nearly cured but Dick has given out and is sinking toward alcoholism. . . . His hold is broken, the transference [to him] is broken. He goes away. He has been used by the rich family and cast aside."

Because everyone in the novel has either abandoned Dick's world, like Abe North, or consumed Dick's world for its restorative sustenance before using the strength thus gained to revel in the Barban-Warren world, like Nicole, nobody really recognizes what a self-sacrificial and tragically doomed healer Dick is. What they see, like Rosemary (the importance of whose point of view becomes increasingly apparent because it is collectively representative), are the exquisite surfaces. Like Rosemary, most of the book's people respond "wholeheartedly to the expensive simplicity of the Divers, unaware of its complexity and lack of innocence, unaware that it was all a selection of quality rather than quantity from the run of the world's bazaar; and that the simplicity of behavior also, the nursery-like peace and good will, the emphasis on the simpler virtues, was part of a desperate bargain with the gods and had been attained through struggles she could not have guessed at" (21).

But otherwise, in the new age of selfishly liberated gratifications, one finds the brute simplicities of Tommy's world. Ironically, absence of those brute simplicities in such an age leaves a devitalized intellectualism without moral point or any purpose wider than one's individual careerism or pleasures, in which clashing sexual identities can only pretend to civilization without really having it. To illustrate Fitzgerald uses the McKiscos as counterparting foils for the Divers. McKisco, the ersatz man and ersatz writer whose name sounds like "a substitute for gasoline or butter," has only an ersatz mind and an ersatz culture. He is superficially like Dick in that he too creates his wife's world, but his ministrations are only the claustrophobic imposition of male domination. "Obviously he had created his wife's world, and allowed her few liberties in it" (9–10). He can be merely an inversion, a pastiche of Dick. McKisco is a repressive jailer. He is all talk. His long tongue treatments doctor nothing. It is inevitable that the marital relationship between Albert and Violet McKisco should include a pathetic and disproportionate dose of guerilla warfare, and that the uneasy but incessantly nagging rebelliousness of Violet should aptly endanger Albert's life by causing the duel with Tommy. In the fruitlessness of that marriage, husband and wife are robbed of their manhood and womanhood:

> "The trouble was I suggested the duel [said McKisco]. If Violet had only kept her mouth shut I could have fixed it. Of course even now I can just leave, or sit back and laugh at the whole thing—but I don't think Violet would ever respect me again."
>
> "Yes she would," said Rosemary. "She'd respect you more."
>
> "No—you don't know Violet. She's very hard when she gets an advantage over you. We've been married twelve years, we had a little girl seven years old and she died and after that you know how it is. We both played around on the side a little, nothing serious but drifting apart—she called me a coward out there tonight." (46)

Violet and Albert fight constantly. She throws sand in his face; in an expression of his "maleness" as well as his "civilization," he sits on her and rubs her face in the sand for revenge. What he needs is both the simpler maleness of Barban and the more complex civilization of Diver. He receives some of the former in the duel and is in part matured by it. At least he comes into enough manhood to know his very real limitations, the real smallness of his talent beneath the pufferies that admiring critics pile on him in the popular literary success he eventually achieves.

Barban needs McKisco's respect for ideas, confused though it is. McKisco needs Barban's strong sunlight: the duel was "the first thing he had ever done in his life. Actually he was one of those for whom the sensual world does not exist, and faced with a concrete fact he brought to it a vast surprise" (47). Dick had never denied the sensual. He tried to channel it into a road to health. In his world of virtues and graces, the leadership of the man, the kindly bullying, is neither arrogance nor insecurity, but a means toward dependable identity. Under the umbrella of Dick's values, Nicole, Rosemary, and Mary North had a cheerful and refreshing resemblance. "Their point of resemblance to each other, and their difference from so many American women, lay in the fact that they were all happy to exist in a man's world—they preserved their individuality through men and not by opposition to them" (53). In the world of *Tender Is the Night* women are frightened by those men who, like Abe, are "gigantic" in their "wreck, . . . dominating [them] with his presence, his own weakness and self-indulgence, his narrowness and bitterness." And then civilized "Dick Diver came and brought with him a fine glowing surface on which the three women sprang . . . with cries of relief. . . . Now, for a moment they could disregard the spectacle of Abe's gigantic obscenity" (82–83). Abe, indeed, had just proclaimed himself tired of women's worlds. But in Dick's world it is man's responsibility to give women the freedom that comes from the absolute reliability of their men. "Up to a point that was right: men were for that, beam and idea, girder and logarithm" (190). In Fitzgerald's context men and women should be "opposite and complementary," and when they become "the drought in the marrow" of each other's bones, when they become the same, "one and equal," identity disintegrates (190). Infantile status and behavior then come to characterize sexual roles in the new freedom and power of the babies.

When Rosemary falls in love with Dick, she is on a nursery footing partly because she is still a baby and partly because she sees so much of her mother in Dick. At the conclusion of Dick's successful replacement of her father, Nicole is "afraid of what the stricken" and used-up husband-doctor "would feed on while she must still continue her dry suckling at his lean chest" (279). Mrs. Speers labors to give Rosemary freedom from dependence on her. "Mrs. Speers felt that it was time . . . [Rosemary] were spiritually weaned; it would please rather than pain her if this somewhat bouncing, breathless and exigent idealism would focus on something except herself" (13). Dick labors for similar weaning and independence for Nicole. What dismays and disgusts Dick is the irresponsible avidity with which Nicole eagerly leaps from him after she has used him up. Finally, the only real difference between Nicole and Baby in the brave new world is that Nicole has suffered and is more grateful to Dick than her sister is. The disciplined Rosemary who had made *Daddy's Girl* has become a citizen of the unisex baby world. "You'd never know Mama's little girl," says Collis Clay. "I mean she was so carefully brought up and now she's a woman of the world—if you know what I mean" (208). Mama's girl had become an economic boy in a success that was the mindless product of a civilization in which a Shirley Temple model baby becomes the national redeemer-hero, the builder-out of broken sides:

> There she was—the school girl of a year ago, hair down her back and rippling out stiffly like the solid hair of a tanagra figure; there she was—*so* young and innocent—the product of her mother's loving care; there she was—embodying all the immaturity of a race, cutting a new cardboard doll to pass before its empty harlot's mind. . . .
>
> Daddy's girl. Was it a 'itty-bitty bravekins and did it suffer? Ooo-ooo-tweet, de tweetest thing, wasn't she dest too tweet? Before her tiny fist the forces of lust and corruption rolled away; nay, the very march of destiny stopped, inevitable became evitable, syllogism, dialectic, all rationality fell away. (68–69)

The baby who becomes the queen of a nursery nation so unlike the realm of sane, "nursery-like peace and good will" (21) under Dick's beach umbrellas is consummately characterized by Baby Warren, who takes over Daddy's male fortune and power. Baby is the adult in charge of the family, and as the man of the family she is unfulfilled as a woman, incomplete as a female. There is "something wooden and onanistic about her" (152), and she exhibits an automatic "impetus that sent her out vagrantly toward all new men, as though she were on an inelastic tether and considered that she might as well get to the end of it as soon as possible. She crossed and recrossed her knees frequently in the manner of tall restless virgins" (151). A "tall, fine-looking" creature just like her daddy, "Baby had certain spinsters' characteristics—she was alien from touch, she started if she was touched suddenly, and such lingering touches as kisses and embraces slipped directly though the flesh into the forefront of her consciousness. She made few gestures with her trunk, her body proper—instead she stamped her foot and tossed her head. . . . She relished the foretaste of death, prefigured by the catastrophes of friends" (172).

Coming to Dick's aid when he is beaten and imprisoned by the Italian police, she takes control, menacing and browbeating the carabinieri. In her snobbish gentility she would abhor the "larks" that land a Lady Caroline Sibley-Biers in trouble with the police. But the summation of the world of what old Gausse calls "this sort of woman," Baby is merely the ultrarespectable version of what Sibley-Biers represents. In her awareness of her patriarchal power, she tries to play the man's old public role, insisting on her privileges and the world's proprieties. But it's a farce, an ignorant imitation, for all that remains are empty formalisms. She takes the "refined" English manner as the ne plus ultra of the great world to which she belongs, and in this, like *Daddy's Girl*, Baby becomes part of Fitzgerald's intricate interlinking of the breakdown of sexual identities with the breakdown of national identities. When Baby comes to the American embassy to get help for Dick, her own sense of identity is momentarily lost in her consternation, and the male, official representative of the United States of America is given an identity characterized by a nightly cosmetic routine ordinarily associated with women:

> On an upper landing, just roused from sleep and wrapped in a white embroidered Persian robe, stood a singular young man [the ambassador]. His face was of a monstrous and unnatural pink, vivid yet dead, and over his mouth was fastened what appeared to be a gag. When he saw Baby he moved his head back into a shadow.
>
> "What is it?" he repeated. Baby told him, in her agitation edging forward to the stairs. In the course of her story she realized that the gag was in reality a mustache bandage and that the man's face was covered with pink cold cream. (229)

Fittingly, Baby's unmannerly wrath is repulsed by the ambassador's English porter, and it is the "English" manner of the ambassador that resists her. "He was of the Eastern seaboard and too hard for her" (230), and as he "maneuvered her to the door for an instant the violet dawn fell shrilly upon his pink mask and upon the linen sack that supported his mustache" (231). By the time she arrives at the consulate, however, Baby is in full possession of her sense of identity. She is a Warren. A female Tommy, she browbeats the consul. She knows how to cut across the manners and proprieties at the same moment that she continues her absurd Anglophilism:

> "We're people of considerable standing in America—" Her mouth hardened as she continued. "If it wasn't for the scandal we can—I shall see that your indifference to this matter is reported in the proper quarter. If my brother-in-law were a British citizen he'd have been free hours ago, but you're more concerned with what the police will think than about what you're here for."
> "Mrs.—"
> "You put on your hat and come with me right away."
> The mention of his hat alarmed the Consul, who began to clean his spectacles hurriedly and ruffle his papers. This proved of no avail: *the American woman,* aroused, stood over him; *the clean-sweeping irrational temper that had broken the moral back of a race and made a nursery out of a continent,* was too much for him. He rang for the vice-consul—*Baby had won.* (232, italics added)

Fitzgerald's presentation of this episode as a reenactment of *Daddy's Girl* models his brilliant and ironic interweaving of the novel's themes and motifs.

Baby always makes the infantile demand of immediate and convenient solutions, just as her father had done. When Baby early had considered care for Nicole, her first thought had been to purchase the necessary professionals and let them take care of the mess. With Baby's endowment-money connections at the University of Chicago, she thought she'd just buy some good doctor for Nicole to fall in love with. "A burst of hilarity surged up in Dick, the Warrens were going to buy Nicole a doctor—You got a nice young doctor you can let us use? There was no use worrying about Nicole when they were in the position of being able to buy her a nice young doctor" (152–53). With the incredible arrogance of her monied smugness, Baby is obtuse enough to advise Dick about the care of Nicole— Baby, who does not even understand that the mess to be cleaned up was of Warren making in the first place. And when Franz proposes the purchase of a clinic,

> Baby was thinking that if Nicole lived beside a clinic she would always feel quite safe about her.
> "We must think it over carefully," she said.
> Though amused at her insolence, Dick did not encourage it.
> "The decision concerns me, Baby," he said gently. "It's nice of you to want to buy me a clinic." (176)

Yet when Nicole is well enough for society, Baby is perfectly capable of disdainfully throwing away the very thing she had bought once it had served its purpose. She superciliously tells Dick that in her opinion Nicole should "get out of that atmosphere of sickness and live in the world"—of proper English society, of course—"like other people" (214).

When Baby bailed Dick out of the Italian jail, "she had the satisfaction of feeling that, whatever Dick's previous record was, they," the crook-fortune, mess-making, incestuous Warrens, "now possessed a moral superiority over him for as long as he proved of any use" (235). When this Baby who inherits the nursery nation speaks of money and of the prerogatives it brings her, she hardens and becomes "suddenly her grandfather, cool and experimental" (176). The distance between the reader's insight into the marriage and Baby's shallowly utilitarian view of it is created by Fitzgerald as a subtle and effective method of suggesting judgments. When Dick muses about the painful progress of Nicole's recovery, he says,

> "It's possible that I was the wrong person for Nicole. . . . Still, she would probably have married someone of my type, someone she thought she could rely on—indefinitely."

"You think she'd be happier with somebody else?" Baby thought aloud suddenly. "Of course it could be arranged."

Only as she saw Dick bend forward with helpless laughter did she realize the preposterousness of her remark. "Oh, you understand," she assured him. "Don't think for a moment that we're not grateful for all you've done. And we know you've had a hard time—" (215)

The nature of her gratitude becomes clear when she is annoyed that Dick doesn't know how to play the English game of manners and have the "delicacy" (312) to clear out without being seen when he has to take leave forever of his wife, his children, and his life. When Nicole protests that Dick is not to be simply discarded like an inconvenient leftover and that he did, after all, devote all his attention during six years of marriage to protecting and curing her, Fitzgerald gives Baby the perfect response: "Baby's lower jaw projected slightly as she said: 'That's what he was educated for'" (312).

Utilizing ship names, as he did with the *Tuolomee* in *The Great Gatsby*, Fitzgerald epitomizes Baby's world of predators with the name of the boat that tows Dick to humiliation on the aquaplane. The boat in attendance on the public disclosure that Dick is no longer strong and is no longer the good diver-swimmer that he was when he was differentiated from the raw-skinned newcomers at his beach is the *Baby Gar.* For Fitzgerald the new predatory world is one in which women demand the prerogatives they had derived from male support in the old relationship of the sexes, while repudiating the roles that had made the old relationship what it was. They want men to put the world in place for them while denying men the old importance of identity that had accompanied their function. So the men become vulnerable in their pride, the fact of which becomes invisible to the obtuse Babies, who only have to boss and order and demand—and flourish their male checkbooks. At one point, without directly saying the words, Baby indicates to Dick that

"We own you, and you'll admit it sooner or later. It is absurd to keep up the pretense of independence."

It had been years since Dick had bottled up malice against a creature. . . . Now he lost his temper at Baby and simultaneously tried to coop it up within him, resenting her cold, rich insolence. It would be hundreds of years before any emergent Amazons would ever grasp the fact that a man is vulnerable only in his pride, but delicate as Humpty Dumpty once that is meddled with—though some of them paid the fact a cautious lip-service. Dr. Diver's profession of sorting the broken shells of another sort of egg had given him a dread of breakage. But:

"There's too much good manners," he said on the way back to Gstaad in the smooth sleigh.

"Well, I think that's nice," said Baby.

"No, it isn't," he insisted to the anonymous bundle of fur. "Good manners are an admission that everybody is so tender that they have to be handled with gloves. Now, human respect—you don't call a man a coward or a liar lightly, but if you spend your life sparing people's feelings and feeding their vanity, you get so you can't distinguish what *should* be respected in them."

. . . "Dick, you've always had such beautiful manners," said Baby conciliatingly [as Dick began to argue with one of her Englishmen]. (177–78)

Defeated by the triumph of the androgynous international baby world, Dick is embittered by the ironic futility of his self-sacrifice. His battle for Nicole's health had been a battle for woman's fully responsible equality and freedom. He had built up Nicole to adult humanity only to have to turn her loose, in her freedom, to the world that is the triumph of the sickness and irresponsibility he had spent his life combating. In his lost war he turns against the appearances, the manners, of what he had been trying to defend (his manners become increasingly rude and hostile), recognizing the rotten reality beneath class manners that are devoid of the morals of virtue.

Dick's lost battle is echoed in the lost sexual war of his brilliant, courageous patient, who lies dying beneath her torture-sheath of excruciating eczema. In the battle of sexual identity she too has fought some kind of campaign for independent freedom and autonomous self-hood, but was not quite strong enough to bear the burdens of the avant-garde. We never quite know what her revolutionary dissent was—whether she was wounded in a war for women's

suffrage, for her art, or for love conventional or lesbian. Dick and
Franz know only that "she was an American painter who had lived
long in Paris. They had no very satisfactory history of her" (183). The
specific is beside the point, and Fitzgerald deliberately leaves it vague.
The only thing we can infer with some certainty is that she was not
merely one of the irresponsible, "liberated" golden girls of the corrupt new world, but that, like Dick, she too had struggled to establish
morally significant adult sexual identity. "I'm sharing the fate of the
women of my time who challenged men to battle," she says (184).
There is a hint that she suffers from emotionally induced symptoms of
syphilis, that she is dying beneath a sexually oriented self-punishment
for something she doesn't understand. Not for a mere libertine's dec-
laration of freedom, for she has "found nothing to blush for since I
cut my wisdom teeth" (184). She either has lost an identity that once
sustained her or has failed to find the new identity that would sustain
her in her battle with men.

> "To your vast surprise it was just like all battles," [Dick] . . .
> answered, adopting her formal diction.
> "Just like all battles." She thought this over. "You pick a set-
> up, or else win a Pyrrhic victory, or you're wrecked and ruined—
> you're a ghostly echo from a broken wall." (184)

She voices what is happening to Dick, who picked nothing less
than the redemption of a world he had believed in for his battle, neither a setup nor a Pyrrhic victory. "I am here," she insists, "as a symbol of something. I thought perhaps you would know what it was"
(185). Indeed he does. What she had sought Dick had sought when he
aspired to becoming the universal healer, "maybe the greatest one that
ever lived" (132). But mechanically, Dick has to find words of treatment; he cannot admit to his ruined patient that she is probably accu-
rate in her self-destructive assessment of history:

> "You are sick," he said mechanically.
> "Then what was it I had almost found?"
> "A greater sickness."
> "That's all?"

"That's all." With disgust he heard himself lying, but here and now the vastness of the subject could only be compressed into a lie.

. . . The frontiers that artists must explore were not for her, ever. She was fine-spun, inbred—eventually she might find rest in some quiet mysticism. Exploration was for those with a measure of peasant blood, those with big thighs and thick ankles who could take punishment as they took bread and salt, on every inch of flesh and spirit. (185)

There is just too much destructive truth, learned bitterly out of his own experience, for Dick to be able to tell it to her. "—Not for you, he almost said. It's too tough a game for you" (185). But she cannot discount her pain. Her pain must be "'for something,' she whispered. 'Something must come of it.'" And Dick replies with the only bit of decalogue left him from another universe, a reply of deepest meaning that remains unheard by the world full of androgynous babies:

He stooped and kissed her forehead.
"We must all try to be good," he said. (185)

Rosemary Hoyt shares with the dying patient the narrative function of contrasting the former world of aspiring hopes and the emergent world of infantile fulfillment. The only fresh innocence that Dick can see any longer in his actual world exists solely in lost youth, *in the memory of the illusions of the future* that existed in the past. And Rosemary and the sun-bright new world are both in the process of shedding their youth. The book's central psychological irony is that the supposedly liberated generation loses its youth to grow up into infantilism.

Rosemary, like Dick, is a disciplined diver. She was "brought up to work" (40), driving herself to illness in her unremitting effort. "One day I happened to have the grippe and didn't know it, and they were taking a scene where I dove into a canal in Venice. It was a very expensive set, so I had to dive and dive and dive all morning. Mother had a doctor right there, but it was no use—I got pneumonia" (17). Dick becomes infatuated with Rosemary precisely because she is the only person who reminds him any longer of the youthful past that imagined a redeemed future. In her youthfulness Rosemary has not yet quite fully emerged into the hardened adult's infantile world of promiscuous gratifications, but with her sunburn hovers on the edge of fresh childhood. Her pinkness is "like the thrilling flush of children after their cold baths in the evening. . . . Her body hovered delicately on the last edge of childhood—she was almost eighteen, nearly complete, but the dew was still on her" (4). And looking at her, Dick "said thoughtfully and deliberately, 'You're the only girl that I've seen for a long time that actually did look like something blooming'" (22). Literally meaning "dew of the sea," *rosemary* suggests youth and memory. Plant and flower, rosemary is considered tonic and stimulating and stands for "remembrance" in the allegorical tradition of flower nomenclature. But there's only one kind of creature that blooming Rosemary can flower into with the nurture of *Daddy's Girl* wealth in a Daddy's Girl world. As Dick increasingly breaks down, what drives him from protective love in his early infatuation with Rosemary's flowerlike freshness to a frenzy of jealous lust concerning defloration is the vision, provided by Collis Clay, of Rosemary playing the new golden girl in the closed Pullman compartment.

> "—Do you mind if I pull down the curtain?"
> "—Please do. It's too light in here" (88).

Frustrated by the painful defeat of his altruistic memories, he sees the precious sweetness of youthful promise consumed with thoughtless greed by all about him. With increasing dissolution and desperation, Dick hungrily lusts for whatever he can reclaim, wantonly falling in momentary love with every pretty young woman he sees. But there is no magical time, place, or self to go back to. When Rosemary was all dewy fresh, Dick had been protective adult. When she had whispered, "Take me," "astonishment froze him rigid" and he had asked in his confusion, "Take you where?" (64). But now both

Dick and Rosemary live in a world of infantile big boys and girls. All Dick claims when he finally claims Rosemary is Daddy's Girl completely grown up into Mama's Economic Boy.

> "Are you actually a virgin?"
> "No-o-o!" she sang. "I've slept with six hundred and forty men—if that's the answer you want" (211).

And tired, used up, out of love, and infinitely older than he had been, Dick finally takes a much older Rosemary amid phone calls, his own jealousy of Signor Nicotera, moments snatched from Rosemary's busy-ness schedules. "She wanted to be taken and she was, and what had begun with a childish infatuation on a beach was accomplished at last" (213).

At last nothing.

For Nicole too the consummation of freedom is the lost residue of love. What shows through Nicole's madness as she comes closer and closer to the final sexual transference that will effect her cure is a growing defiance. Even in the depths of her breakdown at the fair, when she rides hysterically on the small Ferris wheel, as she regains an evil composure her posture is significant. As Dick takes over and assumes responsibility (it becomes harder each time), and gets the children safely out of the way, he and the proprietor of the inn try to right the family vehicle that Nicole has capsized. Dick "and Nicole looked at each other directly, their eyes like blazing windows across a court of the same house." And as "she watched the men trying to move the car her expression became defiant" (193).

In the wreckage of this sexual warfare, all that's left, as in *The Great Gatsby,* is "the foul dust that floated in the wake of" the hero's dreams. "We're all there is!" cries Mary North Minghetti, representative of the brave new "women's worlds." But these worlds are the broken universe inherited from the *fathers,* the hot cosmos that Nicole was born to. When Dick bitterly protests the unearned, righteous, Babyish snobbishness of Mary North Minghetti, Nicole replies with defiant spite, "I like her" (287).

Mary had been a sympathetic character, a charming and courageous woman, when she labored to save Abe and redeem his genius. With the death of Abe Mary is emancipated from her bondage to his drunkenness and despair; but she also surrenders her citizenship in the select world of courage and discipline that had characterized her and that Abe alcoholically had corrupted. Although the function Fitzgerald weaves for Mary is more noticeable in the motif of dissolved national identities, that motif is inseparable from the pattern of sexual identities. Ironically, she finds her "liberty" in the fantastic wealth of an Asian potentate whose customs are based on the complete subjection of women, as typified in Hossain's *himadoun* sisters and in Mary's total fealty.

But it's a small price to pay, for she is no longer tied to a man through the restrictions of the old virtues and graces, and she overlooks the fact that in her new freedom she is more bound than ever. Tragically, the inhabitants of Fitzgerald's brave new world never understand that they have exchanged one set of fetters for another, and, feeling the carefree exhilaration of freedom from moral discipline and responsibility, think they are free. It is telling that Mary's last real encounter with Dick (before she talks with him on the papal rock above the beach as he takes his final leave) is the "lark" she and Lady Caroline Sibley-Biers play, a prank that is fittingly a confusion of sexual identity. Lady Caroline is introduced as the extreme incarnation of the new woman. Her theme song is

> There was a young lady from hell,
> Who jumped at the sound of a bell,
> Because she was bad—bad—bad,
> She jumped at the sound of a bell,
> From hell (BOOMBOOM)
> From hell (TOOTTOOT)
> There was a young lady from hell—" (272)

With her totally and arrogantly callous irresponsibility, Fitzgerald brings to a summary surge the central amoral characteristic of the hot new world. All gilt, she is incapable of guilt: there is a complete "lack, in Lady Caroline's face, of any sense of evil, except the evil wrought by the cowardly Provençal girls and the stupid police" who had caught Lady Caroline in her own fun. Dick is "torn between a tendency to ironic laughter and another tendency to order fifty stripes of the cat and a fortnight of bread and water" (304). "'It was merely a lark,' said Lady Caroline with scorn" (303), a lark that sums up the confusion of girlboybabies: Mary and Lady Caroline had been "boys," dressed up in French sailor suits, picking up girls to bring to a hotel room. In Lady Caroline there is not even a vestige, as there still is in Mary, of gratitude for the good doctor who helps her in her plight. She owes nothing to anyone: the extreme extension of Baby and the new Nicole, she disclaims any claims on her. She will not even repay old Gausse, the hotelier, the money he has put up as a bribe to get her out of jail. Mary is panic-stricken lest she be exposed. All depends on her new identity in her new world, and that, like her national identity, is now hard to establish at best. When Dick asks the chief of police if the identities of Mary and Lady Caroline are known—"you have their Cartes d'Identite?"—the officer replies, "They had none. They had nothing" (305).

"I have never seen women like this sort of woman," says old Gausse after Sibley-Biers, "swollen with righteousness," refuses to repay the bribe money. "I have known many of the great courtesans of the world, and for them I have much respect often, but women like these women I have never seen before" (306). And to that have the identity and heritage of Abe and Mary of the North descended.

6

National Identities

Fitzgerald complicates national identities in the same way and for the same purposes of moral evaluation that he deliberately confuses sexual identities. One of his methods is to yoke disparate names and origins. Señor Luis Campion speaks with a British vocabulary and accent; Mrs. Abrams "was not a Jewess, despite her name" (7). Nick Carraway's old timetable, with its hilarious and significant names in *The Great Gatsby*, parallels Tommy Barban's Paris edition of the New York *Herald*, wherein some representatively anomalous creatures are named.

> "Well, what nationality are these people?" [Tommy]. . . demanded, suddenly, and read with a slight French intonation, "'Registered at the Hotel Palace at Vevey are Mr. Pandely Vlasco, Mme. Bonneasse'—I don't exaggerate—'Corinna Medonca, Mme. Pasche, Seraphim Tullio, Maria Amalia Roto Mais, Moises Teubel, Mme. Paragoris, Apostle Alexandre, Yolanda Yosfuglu and Geneveva de Momus!'" (18)

From "the news of Americans" in the previous week's paper, Nicole and Dick add "Mrs. Evelyn Oyster" and "Mr. S. Flesh" (18). Abe's very American Mary North, "the daughter of a journeyman paper-hanger" from Newark, New Jersey, "and a descendant of President Tyler" (53), becomes the Contessa di Minghetti. But that apparently Italian title turns out to be too clear and simple an identity. The Conte di Minghetti "was not quite light enough to travel in a pull-man south of Mason-Dixon." His "wealth flowed from his being a ruler-owner of manganese deposits in southwestern Asia." He "was of the Kybel-Berber-Sabaean-Hindu strain that belts across north Africa and Asia," and the peerage to which this African-Asian-Hindu belongs is conferred by "a papal title" (258–59). How's that, Fitzgerald seems to be saying, for a confusion of national identities?

Europeans and Americans become intermingled as members of class rather than of nations. As Chicago-bred Baby Warren fixes on the English for all that is proper, Dick, who has the only constantly trust-worthy moral view of the creatures who inhabit the novel, begins to find "something antipathetic in the English lately. England was like a rich man after a disastrous orgy who makes up to his household by chatting with them individually, when it is obvious to them that he is only trying to get back his self-respect in order to usurp his former power" (195). For Baby the world is divided into "the English" (the novel is full of instances of Fitzgerald's Irish willingness to use "the English" as representatives of greed and arrogant stupidity) and the hired hands, and like all babies, Baby cannot be bothered with respon-sible distinctions. As for the social caste that Baby admires, Dick "had long concluded that certain classes of English people lived upon a con-centrated essence of the anti-social that, in comparison, reduced the gorgings of New York to something like a child contracting indigestion from ice cream" (304). Baby's young Englishman at Gstaad is a ruddy ass, braying sophomorically Hemingwayesque noises about loving his friend the more he hit him, and betraying his pretentious limitations at every hee-haw. The sociopathically decadent Lady Sibley-Biers is a notorious representative of "the English." Yet when Baby thinks that for appearances' sake Nicole is well enough to stop living at a clinic, she does not mean that Nicole should retire to the protective world Dick has built in the Villa Diana. There are no fashionable people there. Baby repudiates "that hermit's life on the Riviera, up on a hill away from anybody. I didn't mean to go back to that life. I meant, for instance, London. The English are the best-balanced race in the world."

"They are not," [Dick] . . . disagreed.

"They are. I know them, you see. I meant it might be nice for you to take a house in London for the spring season—I know a dove of a house in Talbot Square you could get, furnished. I mean, living with sane, well-balanced English people." (214)

All nationalities merge for her in an arrogantly oversimplified identity of class status. When she sizes up Franz, she makes "a quick examination of him and, failing to find any of the hall-marks she respected, the subtler virtues or courtesies by which the privileged classes recognize one another, treated him thereafter with her second manner" (173). The fact that Franz helped cure Nicole is not a consideration: that was the service job for which his international class was created.

Fitzgerald's notes for *Tender Is the Night* indicate that puns on names are intentionally significant (like *Barban* for *barbarian*). They suggest the phoniness of pretentious appearances in a counterfeit world and indicate and satirize identities. So the male Campion (*camping* was contemporary slang for homosexuality) chums around with a Royal Dumphrey, and Barban, who combines warfare with loss of national identity, insists that American Nicole speak French. Half American, half French, he asserts that "I was educated in England and since I was eighteen I've worn the uniforms of eight countries" (30). Hollywood is transported to the Riviera in a studio inhabited by French extras, American managers, an Italian star, and an English director in a setting that is a surreal displacement of all identity. When Rosemary visits the studio, we see "a decayed street scene in India, a great cardboard whale, a monstrous tree bearing cherries as large as basketballs," all "as autochthonous as the pale amaranth, mimosa, cork oak, or dwarfed pine" (22). On the set Rosemary meets Earl Brady, a Cockney director who is filming a scene with a French actor and an American actress. Amid the distortions and confusions, "here and there figures spotted the twilight, turning up ashen faces to her like souls in Purgatory watching the passage of a mortal through" (23). When Rosemary, "from the middle of the [American] middle class" (53), is last seen in the novel, she is considering marriage to the strutting European sheik, Signor Nicotera.

When Abe North returns to Paris, in a queer foreshadowing of what Mary's identity will become he is mistakenly called "Mr. Afghan North" by a *sergent de ville* who insists that Afghan's "carte d'identité has been seen" (96). The black restaurateur, Freeman, is confused in Abe's mix-up with an anonymous black, who in turn is mistaken for another American black (105) misidentified to the police by yet another American black, who is referred to by Abe as "a Negro from Copenhagen" and later introduced by Abe "as Mr. Peterson of Stockholm" (105); the beginnings of the confusion are phoned up by the concierge as the report of "Meestaire Crawshow, un nègre" (97). Tommy Barban, recovering from the ministrations of a Warsaw surgeon, turns up in the Marienplatz in Munich with a white guard Russian prince he has rescued, both of them wearing clothes made by "Pilsudski's own tailor" (197).

Like the life of Tommy's czarist Prince Chillicheff in the Soviet Russia where Tommy received his skull wound, national identities are marginal. Humanity itself is marginal in a hot new world where stocks, futures, and identities are bought on unregulated margin. Lady Caroline Sibley-Biers (she is sibling to all the girlboybabies, and her life is the bier of all the broken decalogues) is introduced on a stockbroker's yacht named the *Margin*, owned by a money-man named Golding. When Rosemary hears that Dick is "not received anywhere any more," the news comes fittingly from the mouths of "some State Department people, . . . Europeanized Americans who had reached a position where they could scarcely have been said to belong to any nation at all." In this warren of a world, where people "belong" only to a "Balkan-like state composed of similar citizens—the name of the ubiquitously renowned Baby Warren had occurred" (287), and Rosemary had heard about Dick.

In examining the significance of the confusion of national and sexual identities in *Tender Is the Night*, we should note the frequency with which the liberation of the new Amazon from the old virtues and graces is cast in terms of combat and warfare. The warfare Fitzgerald is writing about is not merely a matter of old nationalisms. The issues that he, in his time, had to work with are vehicles for the eternal human matter of moral responsibility in a moment of battle between a dying old world and an anarchic new one. Fitzgerald weaves the idea of broken decalogues and identities through a metaphor of war that becomes the novel's summary motif.

7

War and Identity

When the babygirl goddess, Rosemary, is introduced, her hair is called "an armorial shield" of "lovelocks" and "gold" (3). Tommy, the most denationalized figure in the book, is totally and constantly associated with wars and the uniforms of various nations; the moral significance of his multiple identities lies in his political indifference to everything but his own immediate interests.

> "Don't you care what you fight for?" asks Rosemary.
> "Not at all—so long as I'm well treated," Tommy responds (30).

Overtones of war permeate the book's language in almost every event. The blacks involved in "Afghan" North's deadly fiasco are referred to as tracking war parties of hostile and friendly Indians (110). The carefree young people of the postwar world are called "the *Sturmtruppen* of the rich" (171), as the new women beyond Gausse's comprehension are called "emergent Amazons" (177). At one of Dick's parties Abe North introduces people as "Major Hengest and Mr. Horsa" (77), and the party reaches its peak—or nadir—of hilarity when the revelers rouse a hotel staff for emergency service to "General Pershing," played by Abe, while the tired, befuddled waiters "stood up and mumbled remembered fragments of war songs at him" (78). The self-sacrificial love that was once made possible by established and dependable identities meets its death in a world war that silhouettes the foreground action of the Divers' war.

It is at the moment of the dying of the old world and the birth of the new that Dick Diver is thrust among the blurred identities of the international scene. Revisiting a battlefield with Abe and Rosemary, Dick mourns a terrible loss. "'All my beautiful lovely safe world blew itself up here with a great gust of high explosive love,' Dick mourned persistently" as he identified what it was that died in those trenches:

> This western-front business couldn't be done again, not for a long time. The young men think they could do it but they couldn't. They could fight the first Marne again but not this. This took religion and years of plenty and tremendous sureties and the exact relation that existed between the classes. The Russians and Italians weren't any good on this front. You had to have a whole-souled sentimental equipment going back further than you could remember. You had to remember Christmas, and postcards of the Crown Prince and his fiancée, and little cafés in Valence and beer gardens in Unter den Linden and weddings at the mairie, and going to the Derby, and your grandfather's whiskers. . . This kind of battle was invented by Lewis Carroll and Jules Verne and whoever wrote Undine, and country deacons bowling and marraines in Marseilles and girls seduced in the back lanes of Wurtemburg and Westphalia. Why, this was a love battle—there was a century of middle-class love spent here. This was the last love battle. (57)

At the moment Dick makes this speech, he admits he is a romantic. He does not yet know the truth of his own statement. As yet only partly ruined, he still thinks he believes in the new world that has emerged from the war. He still believes in the healings and freedoms and millennial possibilities so glowingly described in all the rhetorical promises for which his generation fought its indescribable "last love battle."

Even later, when Rosemary's progress has deepened his growing disquietude, he still tries to believe in the new world. In a restaurant Dick, Nicole, and Rosemary observe a table of "gold star muzzers," come to visit their sons' graves.

> Over his wine Dick looked at them again; in their happy faces, the dignity that surrounded and pervaded the party, he perceived all the maturity of an older America. For a while the sobered women who had come to mourn for their dead, for something they could not repair, made the room beautiful. Momentarily, he sat again on his father's knee, riding with Moseby while the old loyalties and devotions fought on around him. Almost with an effort he turned back to his two women at the table and faced the whole new world in which he believed.
> —Do you mind if I pull down the curtain? (100–101)

Fitzgerald at once associates the gold star mothers with a deep nostalgia, the memory of lost, irretrievable, and younger days. The old time offers the one fixed point of stable identity in the whirling horizon that opened after the war. And by immediately juxtaposing the evocation of the gold star mothers with the dissonant effect of "Do you mind if I pull down the curtain?" Fitzgerald creates the reader's comprehension of why it is beginning to be "an effort" for Dick to continue to believe in the glorious new world made possible by the butchery and love-sacrifice in the battlefields.

Until Dick is ruined—he had always known that he needed a little ruin and that the price of his intactness was incompleteness—he cannot know in his bones the extent of the truth he was uttering during his visit to the trenches. And how he will know it at the graveside of his father, when he buries the departed old time of youthful belief and decalogues of virtue and grace. But until he truly and profoundly recognizes the nature of the new world that has replaced the old one, his nostalgic sense of the past is marred by a faintly professional sentimentality that tends to reduce history to one of his therapeutically ego-soothing, sensitive performances as the unparalleled social host. The reader is grateful for Abe's puncturing what is left of the sentiment and idealistic illusion that are beginning to disappear from Dick's vision:

"Suddenly a shower of earth and pebbles came down on" Dick and Rosemary,

> and Abe yelled from the next traverse:
> "The war spirit's getting into me again. I have a hundred years of Ohio love behind me and I'm going to bomb out this trench." His head popped up over the embankment. "You're dead—don't you know the rules? That was a grenade" (57–58).

The reader is grateful because at this point Dick's profound truth is still merely nostalgic. He has not yet measured the meanings of nostalgia—as how bitterly he will—on the scales of his own ruin: "indeed, he had made a quick study" of the whole battlefield, "simplifying it always until it bore a faint resemblance to one of his own parties" (59).

Nevertheless, Dick carries on his own war of love and discipline against the forces of disintegration. But he makes a fatally exhausting expenditure of his creative energies in a war not worth waging and impossible to win. Because his idealistic faith and illusions prolong his misperception of the moral nature of the identities emerging in the new world, he spends too much of himself before he sees that he has not been a savior but has been used merely as a hired hand, a combination nursemaid, janitor, and master to the revels of the rich. The contempt and loathing he finally comes to feel for a corrupt society and its representatives are equaled only by the internal disdain and ridicule he finally comes to feel for himself. But before the arrival of that silent, internal, bitter, hilarious laughter that characterizes Dick at the end of the novel, the specifics that go into the development of that recognition are the many instances of Dick's sensitive social function as an entertaining soother and healer of egos blurred by a combat of values. As Dick simplified the war for Rosemary until it bore a faint resemblance to one of his own parties, so Fitzgerald deftly casts Dick's parties in imagery suggestive of war. Observing one of Dick's parties in full swing, Rosemary admired how Dick's "technic of moving many varied types, each as immobile, as dependant on supplies of attention as an infantry battalion is dependant on rations, appeared so effortless that he still had pieces of his own most personal self for everyone"

(77). At moments when Dick becomes aware of the "waste and extravagance involved" in the use of his enormous talents for the amusement, care, and ego-feeding of the brave new world, he "sometimes looked back with awe at the carnivals of affection he had given, as a general might gaze upon a massacre he had ordered to satisfy an impersonal blood lust" (27).

The morning Dick awakens to hold the discussion about war and battle with his eczema-ridden patient, he has already begun to recognize the attrition of his life. "Dick awoke at five after a long dream of war" wherein "navy blue uniforms crossed a dark plaza" and there were "symbols of disaster, and a ghastly uprising of the mutilated in a dressing station" (179–80). The images of war as a metaphor for the identity-destroying battle between sexes, nations, and generations come to a climax during the scene in which Abe departs from the Gare Saint-Lazare. A casual acquaintance of the Divers, Maria Wallis, an emergent Amazon described as "a tall girl with straw hair like a helmet" (82), shoots down her man. As Dick, Mary, Nicole, and Rosemary watch, horrified, the "young woman with helmet-like hair . . . made an odd dodging little run away from the man to whom she had been talking and plunged a frantic hand into her purse; then the sound of two revolver shots cracked the narrow air of the platform. . . . But before the crowd closed in, the others had seen the shots take effect, seen the target sit down upon the platform" (83). When Dick finds out what had happened, what he reports is significantly apt: "they had an awful time finding out who [he was], because she shot him through his identification card" (84). The tiny, toylike, lady's pearl revolver, the emblem of the emergent Amazon's power, is as potent in the ironically chosen station of Lazarus (no one rises from Dick's dead fathers, and only the representatives of war or of corruption, like Daddy Warren, rise and walk again) as is Baby, Rosemary, or Nicole in the sun-bright new world they own. The two porters who hold a postmortem outside the station sum up the motif perfectly in their excited conversation:

"Tu as vu le revolver? Il était très petit, vraie perle—un jouet."
"Mais assez puissant!" said the other porter sagely. "Tu as vu

sa chemise? Assez de sang pour se croire à la guerre" (86).

["Did you see the revolver? It was tiny, real pearl—a toy."

"But so powerful! . . . Did you see his shirt? Enough blood to make you think you were in a war."]

In its summary symbolic energy the scene, brief as it is, is the turning point of the novel. Until that moment Fitzgerald has allowed the reader to know of Dick's increasing disintegration, but only by seeing into Dick's hidden mind. From this scene on Fitzgerald externalizes Dick's growing defeat and impotence, and allows Dick to be seen for the first time in ineffectual poses and impotent attitudes, which culminate in the *Baby Gar* aquaplane incident. In the Maria Wallis scene, Nicole takes over for the first time and firmly prevents Dick from acting as savior, party director, doctor. Dick's first impulse is to help Maria Wallis. For the first time someone else can do better than Dick; for the first time Nicole herself says so, foreshadowing her transference from Dick. Maria's "sister lives in Paris," she says. "Why not phone her? Seems very peculiar nobody thought of that. She's married to a Frenchman, and he can do more than we can" (84). The war sounds that "cracked the narrow air of the platform" sound the crack-up of morale beneath the manner, a crack-up that is the dramatic function of all the action that makes up the rest of Dick's story.

> Then, as if nothing had happened, the lives of the Divers and their friends flowed out into the street.
>
> However, everything had happened—Abe's departure and Mary's impending departure for Salzburg this afternoon had ended the time in Paris. Or perhaps the shots, the concussions that had finished God knew what dark matter, had terminated it. The shots had entered into all their lives: echoes of violence followed them out onto the pavement. (85)

And later, during "Afghan" North's "Indian war," even Rosemary, "who was accustomed to having shell fragments of . . . events shriek past her head," with a "totality of shock" that "had piled up within her" (85), cried out, "Do all the Americans in Paris just shoot at each other all the time" (111)? Dick, the pacifier who catches the shock of shell fragments from all sides, ironically classifies his own "long dream of war" as "Non-combatant's shell-shock" (180). The greatest shock is to discover that the armaments of the old virtues and graces that blew up with World War I are ineffectual—they are merely auxiliary to the moral irresponsibility of the new world.

Mrs. Elsie Speers is a "gold star muzzer" of that older America. The mother of Mama's girl-Daddy's Girl, she has lost two *soldier* husbands. Rosemary's father had been an army doctor (which says something about "the nursery footing" on which Rosemary falls in love with Dr. Dick), and Mrs. Speers's second husband had been a cavalry officer. Both of these old-school warriors "left something to her that she tried to present intact to Rosemary" (12–13). That something is what makes Dick and Mrs. Speers understand each other. Each recognizes and appreciates in the other the discipline, courage, and responsibility that characterize the old virtues and graces. Indeed, "by not sparing Rosemary, [Mrs. Speers] had made her hard—by not sparing her own labor and devotion she had cultivated an idealism in Rosemary," and Rosemary developed "a mature distrust of the trivial, the facile, and the vulgar" (13). Rosemary Hoyt is prepared by a mother (whose name from a second marriage is itself the name of war weapons) so that "she was protected by a double sheath of her mother's armor and her own" (13). But armored for what by a Mrs. Speers who has been "father and mother both"? Mrs. Speers can no more create the world in which her armed daughter will triumph than Dick Diver, who is father and mother both to Nicole, can create the world in which the daddy's girl he cures, arms, and fortifies will emerge as a triumphant Amazon. Exhausted, both Dick and Mrs. Speers belong to the same other world, and that world is dead. "Mrs. Speers was fresh in appearance but she was tired; deathbeds make people tired indeed and she had watched beside a couple" (25).

Dick and Mrs. Speers cannot plan for themselves or each other in the war of identities and values. Dick saw that "no provision had been made for him, or for Nicole, in Mrs. Speers' plans" (163), which permitted Rosemary her spree with him. "So long as the shuffle of love and pain went on within proper walls Mrs. Speers could view it with as much detachment and humor as a eunuch" (163). Dick saw that

Mrs. Speers's "amorality sprang from the conditions of her own with-drawal. It was her right, the pension on which her own emotions had retired. Women are necessarily capable of almost anything in their struggle for survival" (163). Turned "eunuch" by the struggle, Mrs. Speers tiredly lasts into the new world only long enough to protect the product of her former potency. Then she fades from battle, and it is time for yet another goodbye.

Mrs. Speers tells Dick, "You and Rosemary are the politest peo-ple I've ever known," but she adds that Rosemary means it when she says that Dick is an ideal. Dick and Mrs. Speers can understand each other's dedication and discipline, and, in a passage that recalls Lincoln, Grant, and another, older war, he can be honest with her.

> "My politeness is a trick of the heart," [Dick responded].
> This was partly true. From his father Dick had learned the somewhat conscious good manners of the young Southerner com-ing north after the Civil War. Often he used them and just as often he despised them because they were not a protest against how unpleasant selfishness was but against how unpleasant it looked. (164)

Dick, whose voice has "some faint Irish melody running through it" (19), combines within himself both Rosemary's romanticism ("her real depths are Irish and romantic and illogical" [164]) and Mrs. Speers's pragmatic toughness. The disciplined romanticism that attracts Dick to the young Rosemary's freshness is the common bond all three share, a heritage from the past. In the scene of farewell to Mrs. Speers the references to war and combat indicate a woman with the good charm of an identity very different from that gained in battle by the new world Amazons.

> Saying good-by, Dick was aware of Elsie Speers' full charm, aware that she meant rather more to him than merely a last unwillingly relinquished fragment of Rosemary. . . . If the cloak, spurs and brilliants in which Rosemary had walked off were things with which he had endowed her, it was nice in contrast to watch her mother's grace knowing it was surely something he had not

evoked. She had an air of seeming to wait, as if for a man to get through with something more important than herself, a battle or an operation, during which he must not be hurried or interfered with. When the man had finished she would be waiting, without fret or impatience, somewhere on a high stool, turning the pages of a newspaper.

"Good-by." (165)

Dick's success as Nicole's doctor is his defeat in battle as history's doctor. He is totally used up, like Mrs. Speers. The final instant when his daddy's girl emerges, all cured and new, into her new freedom is a scene of warfare between two worlds. Nicole

began to feel the old hypnotism of his intelligence, sometimes exercised without power but always with substrata of truth under truth which she could not break or even crack. Again she struggled with it, fighting him with her small, fine eyes, with the plush arrogance of a top dog, with her nascent transference to another man, with the accumulated resentment of years; she fought him with her money and her faith that her sister disliked him and was behind her now; with the thought of the new enemies he was making with his bitterness, with her quick guile against his wine-ing and dine-ing slowness, her health and beauty against his physical deterioration, her unscrupulousness against his moralities— for this inner battle she even used her weaknesses—fighting brave-ly and courageously with the old cans and crockery and bottles, empty receptacles of her expiated sins, outrages, mistakes. And suddenly, in the space of two minutes she achieved her victory and justified herself to herself without lie or subterfuge, cut the cord forever. Then she walked, weak in the legs, and sobbing coolly, toward the household that was hers at last.

Dick waited until she was out of sight. Then he leaned his head forward on the parapet. The case was finished. Doctor Diver was at liberty. (301–2)

Nicole was at liberty. In the actualities of history it was no con-test. The war is over, the new world has won, and Dr. Richard Diver, American, is dead. Shot through the identification card. No Lazarus, he.

8

American Identity

In an essay published three years after *Tender Is the Night,* Fitzgerald movingly summed up his lost, young American sense of early promise and romantic hope seen from the nostalgic and international perspective of later years. In that gone world of youthful dreams, the dreamer had envisioned the gorgeous moment of all possible aspirations fulfilled.

> The compensation of a very early success is a conviction that life is a romantic matter. In the best sense one stays young. When the primary objects of love and money could be taken for granted and a shaky eminence had lost its fascination, I had fair years to waste, years that I can't honestly regret, in seeking the eternal Carnival by the Sea. Once in the middle twenties I was driving along the High Corniche Road through the twilight with the whole French Riviera twinkling on the sea below. As far ahead as I could see was Monte Carlo. . . . It was not Monte Carlo I was looking at. It was back into the mind of the young man with cardboard soles who had walked the streets of New York. I was him again—for an instant I had the good fortune to share his dreams, I who had no more dreams of my own. And there are still times when I creep up on him, surprise him on an autumn morning in New York or a

spring night in Carolina when it is so quiet that you can hear a dog barking in the next county. But never again as during that all too short period when he and I were one person, when the ful- filled future and the wistful past were mingled in a single gorgeous moment—when life was literally a dream.[1]

In the unconditional defeat of Dick Diver, Fitzgerald creates his vision of the gorgeousness and the vulnerability of the archetypal American in all his tragic stature. For Fitzgerald that archetypal American is the essence of millennial expectation. He is the distillation of enormous imaginative ability, energy, and infinite hope. As Fitzger- ald said of his most famous representative of the type, Jay Gatsby, "there was something gorgeous about him, some heightened sensitivity to the promises of life." That identification of the essence of the American is Fitzgerald's central purpose in creating a motif of the breakdown of national identities in *Tender Is the Night*. Fitzgerald cre- ated Dick Diver as a highly civilized Gatsby, with a background of the old virtues and graces and with a brilliant education.

In *The Great Gatsby* we see the American in his realization of *dis*illusion only at the very end, in the few moments in which Gatsby, educated by his contact with the Buchanans, walks out to his pool for the last time. And even at that, we cannot be certain that Gatsby either experiences or understands the disillusion. Nick Carraway can only conjecture about Gatsby's perceptions when no message comes from Daisy.

> "I have an idea that Gatsby himself didn't believe it would come, and perhaps he no longer cared," [thinks Nick].
> If that was true he must have felt that he had lost the old warm world, paid a high price for living too long with a single dream. He must have looked up at an unfamiliar sky through frightening leaves and shivered as he found what a grotesque thing a rose is and how raw the sunlight was upon the scarcely created grass. A new world, material without being real.

In *Tender Is the Night* Fitzgerald extends that disillusion into its fullest realization and creates a novel that traces its source, progress, and fulfillment. *The Great Gatsby* traces the evolution of the dream, and the disillusion occupies only a fragmentary moment at the end of the story. *Tender Is the Night* traces the evolution of the disillusion, and the narrative unfolding of the dream occupies only a small part at the beginning of the story. As Gatsby and Diver are completions of each other, *The Great Gatsby* and *Tender Is the Night* together form the all-encompassing Fitzgerald chronicle of the American Dream. By the time Dick looks up at the familiar sky of his fathers' land and bids it good-bye, he has come to recognize the high price of living too long with a single dream. As Gatsby had placed all his youthful faith in being able to remake history and had identified all his dreams in his vision of Daisy, so Dick had taken all his youthful faith in being able to cure the world and had identified all his dreams in his vision of Nicole. It is no wonder that the mortally frail depositories of millennial expectations, the women, are unequal to the aspirations of the dreamer. Their response is summed up in Nicole's rejection of Dick and in Daisy's plaintive cry to Jay during the scene at the Plaza, "Oh, you want too much!" But it is precisely in wanting that "too much" that the gorgeousness of grand idealism shines through tragically as the motivating energy in the illusion-filled foolishness of the American dreamer.

Nicole's final defiance of Dick's American Dream is given familial focus in the scene in which Nicole throws Tommy the jar of camphor-rub for his slight cold. The curative stuff is for the family. It is "extremely rare" and

> it's out of stock down here.
> "Say, there," Dick murmured . . . "don't give Tommy the whole jar—it has to be ordered from Paris." (278).

But Nicole impulsively and irresponsibly tosses the whole jar to Tommy, disclaiming any claims on her. Symbolically, she throws away American Dick, and all his curative, patient years of dedication and ordered care, for denationalized Tommy and all the hot, carefree coming years of anarchic liberties and pleasures.

Although there are more moving scenes in the book, the moment of the camphor jar is crucial. The whole sense of the book is there: the representative Fitzgerald romantic hero moves into the emergent world armed only with his idealism. Adamic Dick arrives in the European world of historical actuality "on less Achilles' heels than would be required to equip a centipede, but with plenty—the illusions of eternal strength and health, and of the essential goodness of people; illusions of a nation, the lies of generations of frontier mothers who had to croon falsely that there were no wolves outside the cabin door" (117). "He used to think that he wanted to be good, he wanted to be kind, he wanted to be brave and wise . . . he wanted to be loved" (133). In the camphor-rub scene Fitzgerald brings together the abandonment of moral responsibility and the essence of national identity: Nicole says of the camphor-rub, "*It's American—Dick believes in it*" (278, italics added).

At the beginning, healthy, young Dick stands out in a Europe "washed . . . by the waves of thunder around Gorizia and . . . the cataracts along the Somme and the Aisne," as he studies in a Switzerland filled with either "sick" or "intriguing strangers" (115). Fitzgerald introduces the young American student as a new man with unlimited possibility ahead of him. Dick learns all there is to know about the science of the day in psychology. Fresh and vital in his confident youth, the strong, life-filled American writes pamphlets in a Vienna that "was old with death" (115). Wrapped in a rug, burning memorized textbooks and notes for warmth, the brilliant young newcomer "had no idea that he was charming, that the affection he gave and inspired was anything unusual among healthy people" (116). At the beginning the creative energies of illusion were strongest. All was health (Dick swam in the winter Danube), youth (he was 25 years old during his stay in Vienna), and promise ("I've got only one [plan] . . . and that's to be a good psychologist—maybe to be the greatest one that ever lived" [132]). That gorgeous moment in youth, when one foresees a fulfilled future as the culmination of the wistful past, is where the envisioned attainment exists, and nowhere else. "Most of us have a favorite, a heroic period in our lives, and that was Dick Diver's" (116).

Setting out with the illusions of a nation, American Dick is warned by a Romanian intellectual that "you're not a romantic philosopher—you're a scientist. Memory, force, character—especially good sense. That's going to be your trouble—judgment about yourself" (117). Rationally, knowing about intactness and incompleteness, he wishes for a *little* of the experience of mortality that characterizes Europe. He wishes to be "faintly destroyed" (116), wishes for "a little misfortune" (117). Aware of his certitude as the source of his hopeful strength, Dick is also aware that his romantic power is somehow American. Conscious of the irony of feeling his strength as a weakness, he laughs at himself for sensing the need for limitation in his "Lucky Dick" (116) excitement of total expectation. "He mocked at his reasoning, calling it specious and 'American'"—his criterion of uncerebral phrase-making was that it was American" (116–17). He knew, though, that Lucky Dick "must be less intact" (116). His youthfully idealistic American sense of indestructability—Franz Gregorovius remarks on Dick's "unaging American face" (119)—allows him to consider an eager, romantic response as crazy as falling in love with and marrying a patient whose life might possibly be his one continuing case.

Possessing the intelligence to realize that his aspirations require at least the faint touch of destructive experience, Dick sees in his "sweet poison," the beautiful Nicole, a double allure: she provides both the romantic challenge and the necessary completing experience. Significantly, Fitzgerald creates Nicole as a signature of decay and destruction, and he also presents her as the gorgeous essence of Dick's American illusions. "Now there was this scarcely saved waif of disaster bringing him the essence of . . . [the American] continent" (136). Her "moving childish smile was . . . all the lost youth in the world" (134), and "there was that excitement about her that seemed to reflect all the excitement in the world" (135). She and Dick play her phonograph, and "they were in America now";

> even Franz with his conception of Dick as an irresistible Lothario would never have guessed that they had gone so far away. They were so sorry, dear; they went down to meet each other in a taxi, honey; they had preferences in smiles and had met in Hindustan, and shortly afterward they must have quarrelled, for nobody knew and nobody seemed to care—yet finally one of them had gone and left the other crying, only to feel blue, to feel sad. (135–36)

The songs emotionally associate American rinky-tink with the transcendent expectancy of youthful excitement. They bring to the young American romantic in Europe the home-flavor of all his dreams. "The thin tunes, *holding lost times and future hopes in liaison,* twisted upon the Swiss night" (136, italics added). Later Dick would learn that his need to serve and be loved was his own essential Americanness, which had found in Nicole exactly the fascination to which he had responded. When called to help Mary Minghetti and Lady Caroline Sibley-Biers out of their arrest, he sees the parallel between his aiding them and his devoting his life to Nicole:

> [H]is self-knowledge assured him that he would undertake to deal with it—the old fatal pleasingness, the old forceful charm, swept back with its cry of "Use me!" He would have to go fix this thing that he didn't care a damn about, because it had early become a habit to be loved, perhaps from the moment when he had realized that he was the last hope of a decaying clan. On an almost parallel occasion, back in Dohmler's clinic on the Zurichsee, realizing this power, he had made his choice, chosen Ophelia, chosen the sweet poison and drunk it. Wanting above all to be brave and kind, he had wanted, even more than that, to be loved. So it had been. So it would ever be, he saw. (302)

When Fitzgerald introduces any similarities between America and Europe at the beginning of Dick's career, those similarities exist where Europe still seems to promise the infinite: "Zurich was not unlike an American city," and when Dick understands why, he sees that it is because Zurich does not have the French topography's sense of finitely "being *here*," but rather leads the eye upward so that "life was a perpendicular starting off to a postcard heaven" (118). Yet even Zurich is not an America of romantic sweep and total expectation, but a place of the "infinite precision . . . infinite patience" of toymakers—a value that Dick, as a scientist, "did not underestimate" (118). Salzburg makes Dick feel "the superimposed quality of a bought and borrowed century of music" (118). Franz, "the third of the Gregoroviuses," is associated with stifling layers of old history: his "grandfather had instructed Kraepelin when psychiatry was just emerging from the darkness of all time," and "the original genius of the family had grown a little tired." If Dick hoped to become the greatest psychologist who ever lived, "Franz would without doubt become a fine clinician" (118–19). The difference between the vision that is catapulted into the future by a past of the most transcendent romantic illusions and the vision that diffidently gropes for the future out of a restrictively overwhelming past—the difference between the Emersonian American and the history-burdened European—is made clear in Franz's response to Dick's assertion that he wishes to be the greatest psychologist who ever lived.

> Franz laughed pleasantly, but he saw that this time Dick wasn't joking.
> "That's very good—and very American," he said. "It's more difficult for us." He got up and went to the French window. "I stand here and I see Zurich—there is the steeple of the Gross-Munster. In its vault my grandfather is buried. Across the bridge from it lies my ancestor Lavater, who would not be buried in any church. Nearby is the statue of another ancestor, Heinrich Pestalozzi, and one of Doctor Alfred Escher. And over everything there is always Zwingli—I am continually confronted with a pantheon of heroes." (132)

Dick's response is sympathetic, but he maintains his American point of view; in his joking reply he continues to associate newness and possibility with the power of America. In an Emersonian vein Dick replies, "Everything's just starting over," and then continues, "I draw military pay all the rest of the year if I only attend lectures at the university. How's that for a government on the grand scale that knows its future great men?" (132).

With realistic equanimity Franz abandons their old scheme for a clinic for billionaires in New York as "students' talk," but Dick "felt vaguely oppressed" by his visit to Franz's world,

> not by the atmosphere of modest retrenchment, nor by Frau Gregorovius, who might have been prophesied, but by the sudden contracting of horizons, to which Franz seemed so reconciled. For

him the boundaries of asceticism were differently marked—he could see it as a means to an end, even as a carrying on with a glory it would itself supply, but it was hard to think of deliberately cutting life down to the scale of an inherited suit. The domestic gestures of Franz and his wife as they turned in a cramped space lacked grace and adventure. The post-war months in France, and the lavish liquidations taking place under the aegis of American splendor, had affected Dick's outlook. (132–33)

But Fitzgerald also suggests another aspect of the meaning of America. Switzerland, for instance, is presented as a bourgeois nation of "diamond salesmen and commercial travellers," using once "bright posters," now "withered away" "to assure the Swiss heart that it had shared the contagious glory of those days" of war (115). Fitzgerald immediately presents the United States as Switzerland's "sister republic," which had merely "bungled its way into the war" (115). The similarities between Europe and the *idea of America* exist where Europe offers occasionally infinite prospects. But the similarities between Europe and the *historical United States* emerging from the war exist where Europe is characterized by Switzerland's commercialism and the superficial sentimentalizing of what once was deep feeling, sacrifice, and hope.

Europe is Vienna old with death, French finiteness, Zurich toy-making, Swiss small-scale petit bourgeois greed, Franz's inherited suit of a life, and the view from his window. Europe is an overwhelming past and a repository of intimidating genius; it is Dohmler's brilliant but diffident professionalism, Franz's middle-class humorlessness, his lack of imaginative daring, his fear of Dick's wide-ranging ideas for *A Psychology for Psychiatrists*. Franz "considered it a rash business," and said to Dick, "You are an American. You can do this without professional harm. I do not like these generalities. Soon you will be writing little books, 'Deep Thoughts for the Layman,' so simplified that they are positively guaranteed not to cause thinking" (138). Franz asserts that his father, were he alive, would fold up his napkin, just so, and would grunt with the hopelessness of trying to explain to a foolish American how childishly wild Dick's sweeping and revolutionary professional perspectives are. But Dick, in turn, is annoyed with the prudential littleness that identifies grand vision as foolishness just because it is grand. "'I am alone today,' said Dick testily, 'But I may not be alone tomorrow. After that I'll fold up my napkin like your father and grunt'" (138).

Europe is the shabby, grubby materialism with which the Swiss sell the Italians their used aerial cables because a funicular accident would be too much of a threat to the tourist business in Switzerland. Europe is the bourgeois drabness and respectability that disdainfully dislike and hungrily envy opulent America.

But Europe is also the realistic wisdom born of an old, tired, history and a magnificent cultural heritage. It is a sophisticated wisdom with which Dohmler refuses to take on all that huge American Midwest for his practice, in direct contrast to the American "commercial alienists." Europe is Freud, Jung, Forel, and Bleuler at the Psychiatric Congress in contrast to the American quick-fix cure-all quacks. In brief, just as there are two Americas and two heritages of the American fathers, so too, in moral parallel, there are two Europes and two paternal heritages. What Fitzgerald does in the breakdown of sexual and national identities in *Tender Is the Night* is to indicate in intricate and subtle symbolic patterns that the best of Europe and the best of America are disappearing in amoral wealth and power, and that the worst of America and the worst of Europe are merging in an international world in which youth no longer represents romantic, creative aspiration and transcendent hope, but trumpets the carefree and irresponsible selfishness that is the death of the world that blew up in the war. That is the story of the book's international setting and of Dick's Nicole.

It was Dick's American uniform that had first attracted Nicole to him (she had never seen one before), but when that young American "essence of a continent" writes letters, the "helpless caesuras" and "darker rhythms" lurking beneath the surface are suggestions of a debased patrimony, as the surface itself is a foreshadowing of the superficial sentimentalities of *Daddy's Girl:* "it was easy to recognize the tone—from 'Daddy-Long-Legs' and 'Molly Make-Believe,' sprightly and sentimental epistolary collections enjoying a vogue in the

States" (121). Nicole's madness distorts—perhaps highlights—the resemblance, but in the context of the cultural values that will be introduced with Rosemary and Baby, it is fitting that the national vogue should be associated with the make-believe that is a consequence of the reality of Daddy-Long-Legs.

Devereux Warren is Fitzgerald's corrupted American, representative of the fallen historical actuality that is indistinguishable from the rest of the fallen world. Warren in his wealth "was a fine American type in every way" (125). The corruption and disease of this long legged daddy are in proportion to America's vast size, wealth, and power. Dr. Dohmler had once thought of settling in Chicago, but when "he had thought of what he considered his own thin knowledge spread over that whole area, over all those wheat fields, those endless prairies, he had decided against it" (127). Appropriately, as Devereux Warren discloses that he was able to get a U.S. Navy cruiser to run the submarine blockade and bring his daughter to Switzerland for treatment, this fine American type adds "that as they say: money is no object" (128). Immediately, American wealth is associated not only with the in-house rape of "the essence of a continent," but also with wealth's outrageous and irresponsibly selfish use of power. Warren prepares a heritage for his baby and his Baby with every unwillingness to clean up the messes he has made and every purchase of others— from doctors to navy officials in wartime—to do it for him. He is about to run away, back to America, when Dohmler insists he must come to the clinic. Warren replies, "But look here, Doctor, that's just what you're for" (129). When the swinishness of Warren's irresponsibly impulsive self-gratification is exposed, Dohmler makes a gesture that associates this "tall, broad, well made" American (125) with the pig warrens of the stockyards:

> As the story concluded Dohmler sat back in the focal armchair of the middle class and said to himself sharply, "Peasant!"—it was one of the few absolute worldly judgments that he had permitted himself for twenty years. Then he said:
> "I would like for you to go to a hotel in Zurich and spend the night and come to see me in the morning."

"And then what?"
Dohmler spread his hands wide enough to carry a young pig.
"Chicago," he suggested. (129–30)

Dohmler "had read about Chicago in those days, about the great feudal families of Armour, Palmer, Field, Crane, Warren, Swift, and McCormick and many others, and since that time not a few patients had come to him from that stratum of Chicago and New York" (127). But the war is scarcely over and Europe is a "mound of debris," and already the "sister republic's" greedy little merchants in Berne and Lausanne "eagerly asked if there would be any Americans this year—'By August, if not in June?'" (147). Even Rosemary and Mrs. Speers are related to imperial power in their Americanness: "After lunch they were both overwhelmed by the sudden flatness that comes over American travellers in quiet foreign places . . . and missing the clamor of Empire they felt that life was not continuing here" (13). Fitzgerald uses every possible characterization at his disposal, even distinguishing between the haughty, impersonal business rush of American trains and the organic quality of French countryside trains: "Unlike American trains that were absorbed in an intense destiny of their own and scornful of people on another world less swift and breathless, this train was part of the country through which it passed" (14). When Dick speaks of Mrs. Speers's "other America" qualities of discipline, responsibility, and hope, he insists that "she has a sort of wisdom that's rare in America" now (37). When Barban wants another shot at McKisco, he insists on a world where the molly-make-believe miracles of *Daddy's Girl* do not prevail: "'The distance was ridiculous,' he said. 'I'm not accustomed to such farces—your man must remember he's not now in America'" (50). With its speed, wealth, and power, American life offers little restfully constant identity. In a restaurant with his party, watching people enter, Dick bets that "no American men had any repose" (51), and as American after American self-consciously fidgets and squirms, he wins his bet. The restaurant party Dick organizes "was overwhelmingly American and sometimes scarcely American at all," but when its American features are identified, the details are those of the tremendously shifting variety and social motion of American life.

> The trio of women at the table were representative of the enormous flux of American life. Nicole was the granddaughter of a self-made American capitalist and the granddaughter of a Count of the House of Lippe Weissenfeld. Mary North was the daughter of a journeyman paper-hanger and a descendant of President Tyler. Rosemary was from the middle of the middle class, catapulted by her mother onto the uncharted heights of Hollywood. (53)

When Fitzgerald identifies the hostess in "The Frankenstein" of an ultramodish modernist apartment that Dick and Rosemary visit, he identifies her as "another tall rich American girl promenading insouciantly upon the national prosperity" (73). The "women's worlds" guests in that apartment are either vicious bitches—American—or distasteful, pathetic girls—American—desperately on the make to bigger and better contacts. Many of the book's motifs come together in this inhuman war place: the inhabitants are either sober sponges—English—or nervous revelers—American; Rosemary finds herself making "a series of semi-military turns, shifts, and marches," and ends up listening to a nasty conversation taking place on "a sort of gun-metal ladder" among women whose heads are like "cobras' hoods," while she is confronted by "a neat, slick girl with a lovely boy's face" (72).

American tourists "promenading insouciantly upon the national prosperity" share a quality of carefree thoughtlessness. In describing the scene of Abe's departure from the Gare Saint Lazare, Fitzgerald offers a snapshot.

> Nearby some Americans were saying good-by in voices that mimicked the cadence of water running into a large old bathtub. Standing in the station, with Paris in back of them, it seemed as if they were vicariously leaning a little over the ocean, already undergoing a sea-change, a shifting about of atoms to form the essential molecule of a new people.
>
> So the well-to-do Americans poured through the station onto the platforms with frank new faces, intelligent, considerate, thoughtless, thought-for. (83)

All that is potentially good in those faces is canceled by the cheerfully mindless irresponsibility that lets others do the caretaking in a world of new people who want only the cardboard heroics of *Daddy's Girl.* The girls that daddies "bring out" in such a world are characterized in Dick's professional visit to "an American girl of fifteen who had been brought up on the basis that childhood was intended to be all fun—his visit was provoked by the fact that she had just hacked off all her hair with nail scissors" (186).

Retrospectively, Fitzgerald recounted the childhood fun in "Early Success":

> The uncertainties of 1919 were over—there seemed little doubt about what was going to happen—America was going on the greatest, gaudiest spree in history and there was going to be plenty to tell about it. The whole golden boom was in the air—its splendid generosities, its outrageous corruptions and the tortuous death struggle of the old America in prohibition. All the stories that came into my head had a touch of disaster in them—the lovely young creatures in my novels went to ruin, the diamond mountains of my stories blew up, my millionaires were as beautiful and damned as Thomas Hardy's peasants. In life these things hadn't happened yet, but I was pretty sure living wasn't the reckless, careless business these people thought. (87)

The outrageous corruptions that the wealth comes from and results in are part of the golden boom that is all, finally, that America comes to mean to the Europeans, and for good reason. When Franz comes to Dick to propose that they open a clinic together, the great question he leads up to in every particle of his being is, Will he be able to get in on all that crass American wealth?

> Franz threw up his chin, his eyebrows, the transient wrinkles of his forehead, his hands, his elbows, his shoulders; he strained up the muscles of his legs, so that the cloth of his trousers bulged, pushed up his heart into his throat and his voice into the roof of his mouth.
> "There we have it! Money!" he bewailed. "I have little money. The price in American money is two hundred thousand dollars. The inovation—ary—" he tasted the coinage doubtfully "—steps that you will agree are necessary will cost twenty thousand dollars

American. But the clinic is a gold mine—I tell you, I have seen the books. For an investment of two hundred and twenty thousand dollars we have assured income of—"

Baby's curiosity was such that Dick brought her into the conversation.

"In your experience, Baby," he demanded, "have you found that when a European wants to see an American *very* pressingly it is invariably something to do with money?"

"What is it?" she said innocently.

"This young Privat-dozent thinks that he and I ought to launch into big business and try to attract nervous breakdowns from America." (175)

When Baby, who financially is very, very responsible, advises that Dick go ahead, she does so in the hardheaded amorality of the Warren certitude that someone else would clean up the mess that is Nicole. "Baby was thinking that if Nicole lived beside a clinic she would always feel quite safe about her" (176). Franz, in his greedy yearning, turns to the opulent America he has come to know through his profession. From his own professional experience, Dick envisions what the Psychiatric Congress will be like, with "the paper by the American who cured dementia praecox by pulling out his patients' teeth or cauterizing their tonsils, the half derisive respect with which this idea would be greeted, for no more reason than that America was such a rich and powerful country" (194). There will be dozens of hangdog, greedy, and mendacious American practitioners who attend the congress only to strengthen their reputations vicariously so that they will be better able to cash in on the lucrative criminal practice. The superior European training, however, would tell; but just as Europeans would be ready to assert their professional superiority, "the Americans would play their trump card, the announcement of colossal gifts and endowments, of great new plants and training schools, and in the presence of the figures the Europeans would blanch and walk timidly" (195).

Franz and Kaethe Gregorovius argue about the Divers, and Franz shouts,

"Hold your tongue—that kind of talk can hurt me professionally, since we owe this clinic to Nicole's money. . . ."

Kaethe realized that her outburst had been ill-advised, but Franz's last remark reminded her that other Americans had money, and a week later she put her dislike of Nicole into new words. (240)

Lurking in the streets of Paris is the "insistent American, of sinister aspect, vending copies of the *Herald* and of the *Times* fresh from New York. . . . He brought a gray clipping from his purse—it cartooned millions of Americans pouring from liners with bags of gold. 'You think I'm not going to get part of that? Well I am'" (309). Perhaps the crescendo of the motif in which the historical identity of America becomes that of loud wealth and power, and an example of Fitzgerald's brilliant skill in weaving subtle symbolic associations, is provided in the comic hotel scene when Tommy and Nicole first bed together. The fornication that announces Nicole's transference from Dick and the America he stands for is accompanied by increasingly insistent references to America in instances of uncouth force and money. When Nicole and Tommy arrive at the hotel "at the desk an American was arguing interminably with the clerk about the rate of exchange" (294). Outside the hotel, a counterpointing noise punctuates all the sounds inside. Like the cruiser put at the disposal of Nicole's influential daddy, the noises are part of the powerful international presence of the U.S. Navy.

Tommy peered cautiously from the balcony and reported:

> "All I can see is two women on the balcony below this. They're talking about weather and tipping back and forth in American rocking chairs."
> "Making all that noise?"
> "The noise is coming from somewhere below them. Listen."
>
>> "Oh, way down South in the land of cotton
>> Hotels bum and business rotten
>> Look away—"

97

"It's Americans." (295)

Insinuated into the scene is an America of brute Warren power and a genteel English hypocrisy that tries to mask the basic facts. Tommy, at least, is a man of few but basic facts. At the moment he tells Nicole about his old Languedoc peasant remedies, she responds,

"Kiss me on the lips, Tommy."
"That's so American," he said, kissing her nevertheless. "When I was in America last there were girls who would tear you apart with their lips, tear themselves too, until their faces were scarlet with the blood around the lips all brought out in a patch—but nothing further." (295)

Such girls are like the two English ladies in their American rocking chairs, pretending to ignore the American navy and the brawling sailors and the sailors' whores. "They're here on an economical holiday, and all the American navy and all the whores in Europe couldn't spoil it," Tommy says in amazement (296). In perfect union with the relationship between the motifs of sexual identities, warfare, and national identities, the sounds of combat—of "two American sailors fighting and a lot more cheering them on" (296)—become an external rhythm for the rhythm in the room, where the new barbarian "doctor" administers his Languedoc peasant remedies to Nicole. The doctor that Warren had bought ("Hit him where it hurts!") is replaced by his daughter ("Yah-h-h!") in the Europe to which she had been brought ("Hey, what I tell you get inside that right!") by a navy that is in attendance as she finally emerges ("Yaa-Yaa!") with a new, hard, fighting man ("Come on, Dulschmit, you son!"). The emergent Amazon takes her regnant place in a world that buys the private services of national armed forces ("YA-YEH-YAH!"), and the sounds of her triumph are the sounds of the instruments of battle: "then a sound split the air outside: Cr-ACK—BOOM-M-m-*m!* It was the battleship sounding a recall" (296). The sounds are magnifications of the sounds that cracked the narrow air of the station platform when Maria Wallis shot her man through his identification card. Unlike Dick's farewells to his lost world, the noises of the departing sailors are the sounds of turmoil and confusion, the gross noises of violent action and the exchange of money, noises whose coda is reached in voices revealing in raw tones the pathetic whorishness that underlies the alluring voice of Daisy Buchanan, that underlies the seductive "low, almost harsh" (17) quality of Nicole's cultured voice:

> Now, down below their window, it was pandemonium indeed— for the boat was moving to shores as yet unannounced. Waiters called for accounts and demanded settlements in impassioned voices; there were oaths and denials, the tossing of bills too large and change too small; passouts were assisted to the boats, and the voices of the naval police chopped with quick commands through all voices. There were cries, tears, shrieks, promises, as the first launch shoved off and the women crowded forward on the wharf, screaming and waving.
>
> Tommy saw a girl rush out upon the balcony below waving a napkin, and before he could see whether or not the rocking Englishwomen gave in at last and acknowledged her presence, there was a knock at their own door. Outside, excited female voices made them agree to unlock it, disclosing two girls, young, thin, and barbaric, unfound rather than lost, in the hall. One of them wept chokingly.
>
> "Kwee wave off your porch?" implored the other in passionate American. "Kwee please? Wave at the boyfriends? Kwee please. The other rooms is all locked."
>
> "With pleasure," Tommy said.
>
> The girls rushed out on the balcony and presently their voices struck a loud treble over the din.
>
> "By, Charlie! Charlie, look *up*!"
>
> "Send a wire gen'al alivery Nice!"
>
> "Charlie! He don't see me." (296–97)

And then, at the moment Fitzgerald has woven the parallel between Nicole and Tommy inside the room and the whores and sailors outside, he makes explicit in one perfect stroke what the national heritage of Daddy Long Legs Warren has come to be:

One of the girls hoisted her skirt suddenly, pulled and ripped at her pink step-ins, and tore them to a sizeable flag; then screaming, "Ben! Ben!" she waved it wildly. As Tommy and Nicole left the room it still fluttered against the blue sky. Oh, say can you see the tender color of remembered flesh?—while at the stern of the battleship rose in rivalry the Star Spangled Banner. (297)

That, says the descendant of Francis Scott Key, is the devolution of the promise of Grant in Galena, of Lincoln, of Emerson, of that gorgeous land of the republic rolling on westward, there, under the night. Except for Twain and Whitman, no other American writer so sadly, with such fascination, repudiation, and longing, has had such an intense love affair with his country, and no writer has calibrated the complexity of the affair as delicately as did Fitzgerald. Alluring Daisy and Nicole both are an America to whose gorgeous promise the dreamer is yearningly alive; Gatsby and Dick are the American, the romantic dreamer; and transcendent, expectant devotion ends in whorish betrayal in both stories.

Fitzgerald associates Nicole with two things in her essential Americanness: a need to be guided and fulfilled, and overwhelmingly alluring beauty. Dick is to redeem that beauty from the ugliness in its life, and Nicole looks pathetically for guidance. "The blind must be led," writes the young Nicole from the clinic. Her home is gone, and she can find hope neither in the past nor in the future. "Here they . . . sing Play in Your Own Backyard as if I had any backyard to play in or any hope which I can find by looking either backward or forward" (124). Dick cannot help but respond when the essence of America in transition, morally and psychologically lost, asks for love. "I think love is all there is or should be," writes Nicole, and Dick, alive to that appeal more than any other, observes to his colleagues, "She seems hopeful and normally hungry for life—even rather romantic" (131). The two of them, "Dicole," stand out against tired, old Europe.

But by the time of Nicole's victory over Dick, there is no moral difference between the American Warren family's triumph and that of the Australian parents of Dick's patient, Von Cohn Morris: "the gross parents, the bland, degenerate offspring: it was easy to prophesy the

family's swing around Europe, bullying their betters with hard igno-
rance and hard money" (254).

Nicole, of course, is substantially different from the Morrises in
that for much of the book she is a sympathetic character and expresses
a sense, derived from intimate experience, of how good Dick really is.
But in the Warrenizing of her essential Americanness is her communi-
ty with the world of Barban, Baby, the hardened Rosemary, Von Cohn
Morris, Caroline Sibley-Biers, and Mary Minghetti—and therein also
is the center of the book's major historical theme. Rosemary's "democratic manners of America" are "superimposed" (8) on French manners, and when Baby searches for help in Rome "her heart lifted at the
word 'American' on the sign" of the American Express Company in
the Piazza di Spagna (231). But it is not the superimposed Americanness or the commercial company in the Spanish Plaza that Dick represents. Dick belongs in the past.

> Only as the local train shambled into the low-forested clayland of
> Westmoreland County did he feel once more identified with his
> surroundings; at the station he saw a star he knew, and a cold
> moon bright over Chesapeake Bay; he heard the rasping wheels of
> buckboards turning, the lovely fatuous voices, the sound of slug-
> gish primeval rivers flowing softly under soft Indian names.
>
> Next day at the churchyard his father was laid among a hun-
> dred Divers, Dorseys, and Hunters. It was very friendly leaving
> him there with all his relations around him. Flowers were scat-
> tered on the brown unsettled earth. Dick had no more ties here
> now and did not believe he would come back. He knelt on the
> hard soil. These dead, he knew them all, their weather-beaten
> faces with blue flashing eyes, the spare violent bodies, the souls
> made of new earth in the forest-heavy darkness of the seventeenth
> century.
>
> "Good-by, my father—good-by all my fathers." (204–5)

Goodbye, America. Goodbye.

9

The Identity of the Fathers

The motif of the fathers is one of the major unifying devices Fitzgerald used to develop the thematic significance of the "Dicole" plot. There are the European fathers and the American fathers, but the distinctions merge, like all other identities in *Tender Is the Night,* into an international amalgam of opposites, the Old World and the New, the past and the present. The older Europe—Franz's forebears, the view from his window, "the Swiss piety of a huge claret-colored photo [of Franz's father] on the wall" (121)—is an oppressive past, but a past of patience, discovery, and honorable achievement at the "heart of the great Swiss watch." But like Dick's American father, that past is faded, as summed up by Amiens, so sadly ruined by the encompassingly significant war. "In the daytime one is deflated by such towns, with their little trolley cars of twenty years ago crossing the great gray cobble-stoned squares in front of the cathedral, and the very weather seems to have a quality of the past, faded weather like that of old photographs" (59). "The original genius of the [European] family had grown a little tired," and it is the American, Dick, who opens the windows in the smoky air of Franz's study and lets fresh air and a "cone of sunshine" into the room (121).

Like the essence of America, Europe is caught in the flux of dramatic change. The change is epitomized by yet another farewell, the departure of the Russian aristocrats, whose princesses write memoirs of "the dim conventions of the nineties" and who have left their "scent . . . along the coast—their closed book shops and grocery stores. Eleven years before, when the season ended in April, the doors of the Orthodox Church had been locked, and the sweet champagnes they favored had been put away until their return. 'We'll be back next season,' they said, but this was premature, for they were never coming back any more" (15). It was not that Fitzgerald associated czarism with the departed graces and virtues. Rather, what Fitzgerald does is to suggest continually in various ways what he had introduced with the motifs of war and nationality: the past is gone. The Russian Revolution would have rung some favorable overtones for Fitzgerald's intellectual readers and for Fitzgerald's own feelings in the 1930s. On the other hand, Fitzgerald did not adopt a doctrinaire approval of the changed new world in the making, no matter how much he was identified with the youth and newness of his day. He assigned an inane defense of the new times to the inept McKisco. But for whatever ills, change is irresistible in the historical moment *Tender Is the Night* presents. In their new money the Divers too represent the change, even in the manners of the very class that survives change because of its great wealth. "At the moment the Divers represented externally the exact furthermost evolution of a class, so that most people seemed awkward beside them—in reality a qualitative change had already set in that was not apparent to Rosemary" (21–22). Rosemary, before she changes into her hard maturity, thinks that the laws of the world of her fathers are still active, but she finds them operative only in her own mother and in Dick. "Now—she was thinking—I've earned a time alone with him. He must know that because his laws are like the laws Mother taught me" (37). In the nursery footing of her crush on Dick, she turns to him as to a father, inversely paralleling the motif of incest, which Dick gently rejects. But as she grows up to become adept in the male world of Tommy Barbans, Earl Bradys, and Signor Nicoteras, her heritage from her fathers devolves into the same kind of world that Nicole inherits from her daddy and grandfather. In one of the book's many quick and subtle thrusts, Fitzgerald even has Rosemary and Nicole discover that parts of their youth touched in the past, and that "gray echoes of girlhood" emanate from two buildings, directly across from each other, where they separately had lived in—of all places— "the Rue des Saints-Pères" (67).

Dick's good American fathers have also devolved to "tired stock," just as has Franz's family; and, like the good European fathers, they raised themselves to the effort of inculcating the old virtues and graces of moral responsibility and hard work.

> Dick loved his father—again and again he referred judgments to what his father would probably have thought or done. Dick was born several months after the death of two young sisters; and his father, guessing what would be the effect on Dick's mother, had saved him from a spoiling by becoming his moral guide. He was of tired stock yet he raised himself to that effort.
> . . . "Once in a strange town when I was first ordained [Dick's father told him], I went into a crowded room and was confused as to who was my hostess. Several people I knew came toward me, but I disregarded them because I had seen a gray-haired woman sitting by a window far across the room. I went over to her and introduced myself. After that I made many friends in that town."
> His father had done that from a good heart—his father had been sure of what he was, with a deep pride of the two proud widows who had raised him to believe that nothing could be superior to "good instincts," honor, courtesy, and courage. (203–4)

The death and description of Dick's father leaves Dick, in his memories, like Fitzgerald in his, "remembering so many things . . . and wishing he had always been as good as he had intended to be" (204).

But the heritage of the good American fathers is buried in the old land of Indian names. What survives are the Mrs. Abramses of the world, who are "preserved by an imperviousness to experience and a good digestion into another generation" (7). And Devereux Warren doesn't die and get buried. "The old boy took up his bed and walked. . . . He was supposed to be dying of general collapse . . . he got up and walked away, back to Chicago, I guess" (251). The corruptions of the

The Identity of the Fathers

American fathers, unlike the virtues and graces, continue to come home in the new world. Nicole and Dick, in a marriage that is a microcosm of the breakdown in the world around them, sit alone when they have learned that Devereux still walks. The music they hear on the phonograph now is not the music that twisted on the Swiss night air so long ago, foreshadowing the wedding of the archetypal American to the essence of a continent. It is now the music of the world of Baby and *Daddy's Girl*. It is "The Wedding of the Painted Doll" (252).

The wistful past is too far buried to be retrievable. Abe ruminates about his own failure and says, "it was such a long way to go back in order to get anywhere" (81). He drinks to regain that long way back, "happy to live in the past. The drink made past happy things contemporary with the present, as if they were still going on, contemporary even with the future, as if they were about to happen again" (103). Dick, increasingly drunk and impotent in his own ruin, continues to struggle.

> He had been swallowed up like a gigolo and had somehow permitted his arsenal to be locked up in the Warren safety-deposit vaults.
> "There should have been a settlement in the Continental style; but it isn't over yet. I've wasted nine years trying to teach the rich the ABC's of human decency, but I'm not done. I've got too many unplayed trumps in my hand" (201).

But Dick is done. Tommy was right—Nicole has too much money. As Dick sinks more deeply into a parallel with Abe's premonitory career, his sadness about an irrecoverably lost past and about talents, futures, hopes, and decalogues broken plays itself out within him against a significant exterior rhythm—one of Fitzgerald's favorite techniques—that is a tired reminder of the war.

> He slept deep and awoke to a slow mournful march passing his window. It was a long column of men in uniform, wearing the familiar helmet of 1914, thick men in frock coats and silk hats, burghers, aristocrats, plain men. It was a society of veterans going

to lay wreaths on the tombs of the dead. The column marched slowly with a sort of swagger for a lost magnificence, a past effort, a forgotten sorrow. The faces were only formally sad, but Dick's lungs burst for a moment with regret for Abe's death, and his own youth of ten years ago. (200)

Sadly and ironically, the wreaths can commemorate only what has been war-lost. The deaths, the old world, the sacrifices somehow have been mislaid a long way back. During Dick, Rosemary, and Abe's visit to the trenches and war memorials, when an American girl comes to place a wreath on her brother's grave she cannot find the marker, for the War Department has given her the wrong grave registration number.

Always the past is misused by the present. Even Tommy's tradition of the duel degenerates into a Gallic squabble about who will pay for the services of the seconds and the doctors. The affluent and irresponsible present remakes the past into anything it wants. When the fully emerged Rosemary meets Dick after so many years, she says, "we're making 'The Grandeur That Was Rome'—at least we think we are; we may quit any day" (207). They make their movie version of the past in a "huge set of the forum, larger than the forum itself" (212). All that's left of the grandeur that was Rome is in the postwar air of the Italian night in which Dick has his drunken fight with the cabbies and cops: "a sweat of exhausted cultures tainted the morning air" (224). No person is exempt and no culture, no empire. If the heritage of the Roman fathers has become the cabbies, the cops, and Signor Nicotera in a phony movie set, the heritage of the fathers of the British Empire has become Lady Caroline Sibley-Biers. "She was fragile, tubercular—it was incredible that such narrow shoulders, such puny arms could bear aloft the pennant of decadence, last ensign of the fading empire" (271).

In a world that misuses whatever goodness is in its past, Nicole becomes adapted to the world of *her* fathers. Dick is tensely casual when he and Nicole sing,

> "Thank y' father-r
> Thank y' mother-r
> Thanks for meeting up with one another—"

"I don't like that one," Dick said, starting to turn the page.

"Oh, play it!" she exclaimed. "Am I going through the rest of life flinching at the word 'father'?" (290).

Time cures all, and time is the great antagonist of romantic readiness. Tired, Dick knows that he can only pretend that the fathers had saved the world for democracy, truth, and goodness, that he can only feign belief "that the world was all put together again by the grey-haired men of the golden nineties who shouted old glees at the piano" (174). But "he had lost himself. . . . Between the time he found Nicole flowering under a stone on the Zurichsee and the moment of his meeting with Rosemary the spear had been blunted" (201). On his mountain-climbing trip as a hopeful young man, he never did get to the top of his mountain, for "at mid-day the weather changed to black sleet and hail and mountain thunder" (202). In the triumph of the bad fathers, change and time defeat Dick's transmission of the virtues and graces of the good ones. When he was completely locked up in Nicole's moneyed world, he had to adapt every bit of his control, order, and talents to her needs, and when he "could no longer play what he wanted to play on the piano, it was an indication that life was being refined down to a point. He stayed in the big room a long time, listening to the buzz of the electric clock, listening to time" (171). No more than Gatsby can Dick turn the clock back, old sport. The good fathers are dead.

10

The Movies Identity

A lot of money can make it seem that one can do anything with the clock. Time can be put on rewind or fast forward; time can be edited: everything can be made to come out right so that youth, truth, beauty, and virtue triumph and we all live happily ever after, getting everything we want in the best of all possible worlds. As Fitzgerald wrote in his wonderful story "Babylon Revisited," "[T]he snow of twenty-nine wasn't real snow. If you didn't want it to be snow, you just paid some money." This millennial American sense of possibility is what Fitzgerald associated with the movies, a debased version of the redemption of history to which Dick's archetypal American identity aspired. A quick and convenient fadeout dissolves all contingent difficulties, and with the speed of light we are free of the preceding events and are in new circumstances.

In the movietime rush of history, as pervasive a motif in this novel as in *The Great Gatsby* and *The Beautiful and Damned*, the Warrens are the ones best able to keep up with time. For Dick, characteristically sensitized to romantic impulses, "time stood still and then every few years accelerated in a rush, like the quick rewind of a film," but for steadily wealthy "Nicole the years slipped away by clock and calendar and birthday, with the added poignance of her perishable beauty" (180). She's satisfied with the beauty that her wealth makes seem imperishable. The world of the golden girl is a world given over to youth.

Fitzgerald sees complex historical revelation in the American obsession with youth, and he uses the golden girl as its avatar and expression. The "women's worlds" from which Abe withdraws destroy the responsible maturity that might make the dreams of the wistful past regeneratingly meaningful. So Rosemary goes from mother-worship and her daddy-worshiping first romance to the hard world of tired and phony love, commercialized sentiment, and the unreality of tinsel and movie sets. She becomes the movie star whose reading materials are "two novels, one by Edna Ferber, one by Albert McKisco" (209).

Not as a movie celebrity, an identity she disdains, but as an all-new-like-a-baby golden girl, Nicole becomes very much a part of the same new "women's worlds." As she looks at her naked body, which she prepares for Tommy, she gives herself "about six years, but now I'll do—in fact I'll do as well as anybody I know" (290). "Attractive women of nineteen and twenty-nine," Fitzgerald observes in his presentation of Nicole, "are alike in their breezy confidence. . . . But whereas a girl of nineteen draws her confidence from a surfeit of attention, a woman of twenty-nine is nourished on subtler stuff. . . . Happily she does not seem, in either case, to anticipate the subsequent years when her insight will often be blurred by panic, by the fear of stopping or the fear of going on. But on the landings of nineteen or twenty-nine she is pretty sure that there are no bears in the hall" (291). The golden girl does not worry about what is buried with all the fathers; she does not try to make time stand still, much less turn the clock back in any moral sense. She is outside of time. The ABCs of human decency are easily forgotten in that terrible "rush, like the quick rewind of a film," that goes on in the history all about her, for what she foresees is a pleasurable continuum of change "peopled with the faces of many men, none of whom she need obey or even love" (294).

But as we remain forever young, a world that nourishes itself on dreams like *Daddy's Girl* will create values no more substantial than its screen images. Its movies become its reality. Actors "were risen to a position of prominence in a nation that for a decade had wanted only to be entertained" (213). To step from movie glory into the sun-bright charm of the dazzling "real" world one gains by movie fame and movie money is only to step back into the moral immaturity and irresponsibility of the movie, the Señor "Real" world. One steps from nothing into nothing. Dick summed up "the subject with a somewhat tart discussion of actors: 'The strongest guard is placed at the gateway to nothing,' he said. 'Maybe because the condition of emptiness is too shameful to be divulged'" (70).

Writing out of his Hollywood scriptwriter's experience, Fitzgerald used the movies as a metaphor for shallowness, tawdriness, and golden illusion. A world of the kids, by the kids, and for the kids is paradoxically the denial and betrayal of the most noble aspirations that youth dreams of. Someone—poor Dick!—must be maturely responsible enough to give real substance and the ABCs of human decency to the world the kids dream. But in a world in which the movie star must eternally preserve the appearance of her dewy youth above all else, time itself must appear to be conquered, and maturity is simply corrupted into the enemy, perishability. For Fitzgerald the great American paradox of millennial expectation is that the very change of identity we seek in wealth—we all can attain the magic-show gorgeousness of movie-star life—is itself the impermanence we flee in the speedily changeful flux of American life. Travel motion becomes a metaphor for the slide of nationality, sexuality, time, and change—fleeting identity in the rush of movietime. Boarding ship, one

> hurries through, even though there's time; the past, the continent, is behind; the future is the glowing mouth in the side of the ship; the dim, turbulent alley is too confusedly the present.
>
> Up the gangplank and the vision of the world adjusts itself, narrows. One is a citizen of a commonwealth smaller than Andorra, no longer sure of anything. . . . Next the loud mournful whistles, the portentous vibration and the boat, the human idea—

is in motion. The pier and its faces slide by . . . the faces become remote, voiceless, the pier is one of many blurs along the water front. The harbor flows swiftly toward the sea. (205)

Movie-set appearances merely mask an ugly reality of putrescence and lost identities. The clinics, like Devereux Warren's handsome appearance, hide a story of swinishness or madness or both. No matter how silly the sickness with which the clients arrive, one doesn't use the word *nonsense* in "a rich person's clinic" (119). Wealth is catered to, ugly truths hidden, so that as in almost all of Fitzgerald's work, money serves as a means to maintain surfaces that protect the rich from the realities of their lives. The world is changed to a movie set—as manipulated, as two dimensional, as false, and as primarily concerned with surface appearances. "No layman would recognize [Dohmler's rich people's clinic] as a refuge for the broken, the incomplete, the menacing of this world" (120). When Warren finally admits his incest, his anxiety is about appearances, and "he seemed chiefly concerned as to whether the story would ever leak back to America" (130). Doctoring the rich, Dick makes a carefully regulated movie-world in which they can ease their broken psyches. In his own clinic for rich babies, "the bright colors of the stuffs they worked with gave strangers a momentary illusion that all was well, as in a kindergarten" (182). Nicole's set designs for the clinic were so good that no "visitor would have dreamed that the light, graceful filigree work at a window was a strong, unyielding end of a tether" (183).

Dick creates revivifying illusions and surfaces for friends and guests. "Then, without caution, lest the first bloom of the relation wither, he opened the gate to his amusing world. So long as they subscribed to it completely, their happiness was his preoccupation, but at the first flicker of doubt as to its all-inclusiveness he evaporated before their eyes, leaving little communicable memory of what he had said or done" (28). Fitzgerald creates a very complex character in Dick Diver. At once victimized by the movie world of wealth, Dick also caters to it. Morally opposed to insincerity, his profession forces him to its practice. Fighting the irresponsibility of illusion, he uses illusion in the struggle to restore responsibility and health in others. Hating phonies, he is part phony himself in his indiscriminate, vast desire to serve.

The Villa Diana, with its "intensely calculated perfection" is like the movie-illusion clinics. Built with Warren money, it is a disguise shielding and hiding sickness. The garden, Nicole's masterpiece, is exquisitely calibrated, and the dinner party in the garden is Fitzgerald's presentation of the movietime loveliness—moon, lanterns, and all— that can be created for Busby Berkeley surfaces that become an entire lifestyle: the table seems to rise "a little toward the sky like a mechanical dancing platform" (34). When Dick awakens to the realization that his dedication to others is transformed by the movietime mindlessness of the Warren world into a merely pimpish service, the movie is over. All the gardens, clinics, villas, manners, and surfaces simply become one more set of sedative illusions for predatory carelessness and decadent rot. Devereux Warren's movie set of a hotel suite is a summation. "The suite in which Devereux Warren was gracefully weakening and sinking was of the same size as that of Señor Pardo y Ciudad Real—throughout this hotel there were many chambers where rich ruins, fugitives from justice, claimants to thrones of mediatized principalities, lived on the derivatives of opium or barbital listening eternally to an inescapable radio, to the coarse melodies of old sins" (248).

When the Diver household detrains, the show of wealth is a movie scene, with all its trunks, satchels, suitcases, servants, sporting goods, grips, packages, and pets: "the village people watched the debarkation with an awe akin to that which followed the Italian pilgrimages of Lord Byron a century before" (258). The Minghetti entourage is there to meet them, and "when these princely households, one of the East, one of the West, faced each other on the station platform, the splendor of the Divers seemed pioneer simplicity by comparison" (259). But on this movie set the Minghetti gorgeousness only signals the silliness and pretentiousness that Mary North has come to exemplify in her new appearances. Like Baby and Mary and, eventually, Nicole, the entire postwar haut monde becomes a movie image of its own status.

With her wealth Nicole subtly and gradually binds Dick into a movie-set world. She can say of Abe what in effect she will even say of

Dick eventually: she "shook her head right and left, *disclaiming responsibility*. . . . 'So many smart men go to pieces nowadays'" (99, italics added). But her responsibility for smart Dick's going to pieces, disclaim it though she may, is enormous. Nicole wants to absorb Dick in ownership, which is the relationship to the world that her wealth has taught her to assume. The bars of gilt metal that Dick uses as paperweights in his study, weighing down his uncompleted manuscripts, are fitting appurtenances indeed: they represent wealth and are empty of value.

> Naturally Nicole, wanting to own him, wanting him to stand still forever, encouraged any slackness on his part, and in multiplying ways he was constantly inundated by a trickling of goods and money. The inception of the idea of the cliff villa, which they had elaborated as a fantasy one day, was a typical example of the forces divorcing them from the first simple arrangements in Zurich.
>
> "Wouldn't it be fun if—" it had been; and then, "won't it be fun when—"
>
> It was not so much fun. His work became confused with Nicole's problems; in addition, her income had increased so fast of late that it seemed to belittle his work. (170)

Not literally in the movies, Dick is of them all the time. He is able to civilize their cardboard quality and crude energy. At the Divers' party, director Earl Brady's "heartiness became, moment by moment, a social thing instead of a crude assertion and reassertion of his own mental health and his preservation of it by a detachment from the frailties of others" (34). Yet even as he ministers, as always he must, Dick sees in the movies all the brainless, philistine harlotry and confusion of values with which the hot new world of wealth breaks decalogues and destroys virtues and graces. He refuses Rosemary's embarrassing offer of a screen test. "The pictures make a fine career for a woman—but my God . . . I'm an old scientist all wrapped up in my work" (70). Appropriately, the scene is enacted in the denationalized Franco-American Films studio during a screening of Rosemary's picture, and, appropriately, Nicole and Mary are derisive but "faintly annoyed" (70) that they weren't invited for screen tests.

But though Dick sees the movies as a summation of everything hostile to his values, his own insidiously imperceptible but continuous engulfment by the Warren world makes him very much of the movies and occasionally makes his pronouncements seem desperate and faintly priggish. In his exquisite social tact he is, as a friend and a host, a movie director; in his professional role he is involved in the rich man's world of corruption and "condition of emptiness." His undoing is his dawning self-realization that in a professional life spent trying to teach the rich the ABCs of human decency, he was in the movies all along. His directorial equipment becomes increasingly useless as with increasing success he teaches his star patient how to do without him. The movie director's megaphone he uses to talk to Nicole across the garden is belittled by the ease with which her unaided voice reaches him. But he "raised it stubbornly" (27). Dick's perfect scenario, the dinner party in the garden, feeds innocence and mindlessness as much as *Daddy's Girl* ever did. It provides illusions by which any identity maintains false dreams, empty hopes, its own self, for an enchanted gorgeous moment.

Naive Rosemary, rich with the wealth of the America she, like the young Nicole, so essentially characterizes, for a moment can movie-believe that she truly belongs to the grand world that, with Baby-like anti-American snobbishness, she associates with the heritage of the European fathers. "Rosemary, as dewy with belief as a child from one of Mrs. Burnett's vicious tracts, had a conviction of homecoming, of a return from the derisive and salacious improvisations of the frontier" (34). So Fitzgerald does not neglect to observe that when McKisco makes it big and Violet enters her longed-for great role—she "was very grand now, decked out by the grand couturières"—she comes to it theatrically with a "soul born dismally in the small movie houses of Idaho" (206). She and Mary Minghetti, like everyone else in the novel, once defined and differentiated by their placement inside or outside Dick's beach world now convivially occupy the same glittering and arrogant Riviera world, in which Dick is no longer received.

When Rosemary first declares her love for Dick, in "the too obvious appeal" Dick is aware of Rosemary's "struggle with an unrehearsed scene and unfamiliar words" (38). As a therapeutic arranger of people's moments, Dick in effect is a director, a force to which the young daddy's girl is attracted. Rosemary "liked to be told how she should feel, and she liked Dick's telling her which things were ludicrous and which things were sad" (58). She weeps on cue during the episode in the Thiepval trenches. And in his own infatuation with Rosemary, Dick observes the bank tellers, deciding which one would least notice his depression. He "decided to go to Pierce, who was young and for whom he would have to put on only a small show. It was often easier to give a show than to watch one" (89). Indeed, Rosemary's first sight of Dick is one in which he "was giving a quiet little performance for . . . [his] group" (6) under the beach umbrellas. When Rosemary weeps, "I've loved you so-o-o," Dick replies, "Not only are you beautiful but you are somehow on the grand scale. Everything you do, like pretending to be in love or pretending to be shy, gets across" (63). And Rosemary, astonished at the words of passion coming out of her, "was calling on things she had read, seen, dreamed through a decade of convent hours. Suddenly she knew too that it was one of her greatest roles and she flung herself into it more passionately" (64). Later, when she reiterated her love for Dick, "It was time for Rosemary to cry, so she cried a little in her handkerchief" (74). When she and Dick are in the Frankenstein apartment, "Rosemary had the detached false-and-exalted feeling of being on a set and she guessed that everyone else present had that feeling too" (71). The "most sincere thing" Rosemary ever says to Dick is, "Oh, we're such *actors*—you and I" (105). When Rosemary thinks of loving Dick "she exhausted the future quickly, with all the eventualities that might lead up to a kiss, but with the kiss itself as blurred as a kiss in pictures" (39).

In Fitzgerald's perceptions his nation's sex-worship and youth-worship were always implicit in a popular and immaturely oversimplifying view of the mythic dream of America, which, in its debased form, was midwifed into full birth by the movies. It is fitting that Rosemary's naive vision of life with Dick is as tenuous as the dissolving image of the final clinch in the happy ending before the lights come on in "the erotic darkness" of the screening room, where Rosemary watches her imaginings. It is fitting that the confused sexuality of identity that Campion represents should be associated with the movies. As he weeps Rosemary thinks of the weeping woman who almost stole the show from her in *Daddy's Girl*. "He was weeping hard and quietly and shaking in the same parts as a weeping woman. A scene in a role she had played last year swept over her irresistibly and advancing she touched him on the shoulder" (40–41). In their unreality the movies become an agent of dissolution of the deepest human moral and emotional reality, making unreality the reality. So when Rosemary overhears the real passion in Nicole's "Oh, *do* I!"—Nicole's response to Dick's question, "So you love me?" (53)—she enters into the genuine fervor with which Dick and Nicole make an assignation, and "she had none of the aversion she had felt in the playing of certain love scenes in pictures" (54). The passions of real love, like moral decency, live secluded in the individual's saintly, angelic "trick of the heart," but Franco-American Films lives "at 341 Rue des Saintes Anges—ask for Mr. Crowder" (53).

The older, experienced Rosemary, returning to Gausse's beach, "was acting amusement, joy, and expectation—more confident than she had been five years ago" (282). When she feels that the reality of the moment with Dick and Nicole becomes uncomfortably revealing of her feeling for Dick, she looks "at the sand exactly between" Dick and Nicole and says, "I wanted to ask you both what you thought of my latest pictures—if you saw them" (287). When Dick tries to explain to Rosemary the difference between truly felt and theatrical reactions to life, the essence of his explanation is that all life is acting but that the difference between life-acting and stage-acting is that the latter burlesques the former. The actress burlesques "the correct emotional responses—fear and love and sympathy" in order "to get the audience's attention back on herself" (288). Nicole, annoyed with everything Dick does lately, listens to the dissertation on responsive acting with mounting impatience. To her the talk is Dick's pontifical showing-off, a dull exposure of the false world of professional responses in which Dick moves. She is forgetful, increasingly so, that *his* directing a carefully staged world has not been of the movies but of a sanative preservation of the perspective and moral order that allow one to come out of despair and into reality. But Nicole, eager to shed

Dick and to reject Rosemary, can see no distinctions through her newly regained white Warren eyes. When Rosemary turns to Topsy and says,

> "Would you like to be an actress when you grow up? I think you'd make a fine actress," Nicole stared at her deliberately and in her grandfather's voice said, slow and distinct:
> "It's absolutely *out* to put such ideas in the heads of other people's children." . . . She turned sharply to Dick . . . without a glance at Rosemary, whose face was "responding" violently. (288–89)

But who is saying what to whom? With the whole world in the fast movie time of the fashionable new beach, with the repudiation of Dick as director, the whole world is at the movies and in the movies. Imperishable Nicole herself "was enough ridden by the current youth worship, the moving pictures with their myriad faces of girl-children, blandly represented as carrying on the work and wisdom of the world, to feel a jealousy of youth" (291). Love is movie love, in which one watches "Nicotera, one of the many hopeful Valentinos, strut and pose before a dozen female 'captives,' their eyes melancholy and startling with mascara" (212). The completeness with which the parallel between the movies, the social scene, and the historical moment is drawn is part of the intentional dying fall that Fitzgerald so compellingly and intricately manages. When Dick sees a pretty young girl in a cabaret, he says, "She looks like somebody in the movies" (222). The response of Collis Clay is hilarious—Collis Clay, that stuffy, harmless, obtuse, perpetual fraternity boy whose last name specifies his body, mind, and soul: "'I'd like to get in the movies,' said Collis thoughtfully" (223). And Collis is not alone. When Dick haunts the vicinity of Rosemary's studio, he runs into the sinister and ridiculous American newspaper vendor whose bible is a newspaper clipping depicting "a stream of Americans pouring from the gangplank of a liner freighted with gold" (93), and who reappears at the moment when Tommy takes Nicole away from Dick. When Dick asks this harbinger of greed and illusion what he is doing in Passy, the man "looked around cautiously. 'Movies,' he said darkly. 'They got an American studio over there . . . I'm waiting for a break'" (93).

Some are in, most want to be in, and everyone is at the movies. Even more improbable people than Clay and the news vendor ludicrously acquiesce in the acceptance of movies as desirable reality. Kaethe Gregorovius insists to Franz that

> "Nicole is less sick than anyone thinks—she only cherishes her illness as an instrument of power. She ought to be in the cinema, like your Norma Talmadge—that's where all American women would be happy."
> "Are you jealous of Norma Talmadge, on a film?"
> "I don't like Americans. They're selfish, *sel*fish!"
> "You like Dick?"
> "I like him," she admitted. "He's different, he thinks of others."
> —And so does Norma Talmadge, Franz said to himself. Norma Talmadge must be a fine, noble woman beyond her loveliness. They must compel her to play foolish roles; Norma Talmadge must be a woman whom it would be a great privilege to know.
> Kaethe had forgotten about Norma Talmadge, a vivid shadow that she had fretted bitterly upon one night as they were driving home from the movies in Zurich. (240)

Hossain Minghetti is curious to know, above all, "about stocks and about Hollywood" (260). Nicole tells Tommy that he looks "just like all the adventurers in the movies" (269). And Tommy replies in kind.

> "I only know what I see in the cinemas," he said.
> "Is it all like the movies?"
> "The movies aren't so bad—now this Ronald Colman—have you seen his pictures about the Corps d'Afrique du Nord? They're not bad at all."
> "Very well, whenever I go to the movies I'll know you're going through just that sort of thing at that moment." (270)

Mary Minghetti makes the movie-life essence clear to Dick: "We're all there is!" she cries to him, having told him that he's no longer the continuing source of entertainment and ego sustenance he used to be.

> "If you don't like nice people, try the ones who aren't nice, and see how you like that. *All people want is to have a good time* and if you make them unhappy you cut yourself off from nourishment."
> "Have I been nourished?" he asked, [as] down the steps tripped Lady Caroline Sibley-Biers *with blithe theatricality.* (313, italics added)

As Dick's career closes down and he leaves the Warren world, so too, the book implies, has time also caught up with the rotten crowd on the garish beach. For a long time there had been "a hint in the air that the earth was hurrying on toward other weather; the lush *midsummer moment outside of time* was already over" (163, italics mine). The hint is not in any facile retributive action, but in the completeness with which the brave new world is given over to irresponsible gratification and mindless corruption—in the completeness with which the fate of Dr. Richard Diver has become the test of his society. In grim historical weather the greatest, gaudiest spree in history is going to dissolve like the unrealities of a movie. Unwritten at the end of the book are the invisible words that bespeak the summation of Fitzgerald's evaluation: *mene mene tekel upharsin.*

11

Sun and Water: Hot and Cool Identities

Dick had re-created his lost, beautiful, safe world in the little beach he made under the umbrellas. But in the new age it had become "perverted now to the tastes of the tasteless; he could search it for a day and find no stone of the old Chinese Wall he had once erected around it, no footprint of an old friend" (280). Fitzgerald uses the beach, swimming, and sunning as metaphors for the uses and misuses of the legacy of the past.

The new people are flabby and pale. They are not swimmers. But those within Dick's world are good swimmers. Dick Diver is an accomplished high diver and aquaplaner, a swimmer in the winter Danube, an aquatic athlete. Ruined though he is, as a member of Dick's circle Abe North is distinguished as a good swimmer early in his appearance in the novel. The new people are hung over and have not adjusted to the sun; Diver's people have grown carefully tanned and healthy on Dick's beach. When the young Rosemary is first exposed to the powerful sun, she is grateful that in contrast to the unregulated heat, the "water . . . pulled her down tenderly out of the heat"—but neophyte that she is, she could swim only "a choppy little four beat crawl" (5). Yet she swims, both on the movie set and at the beach.

Campion, on the other hand, warns people out of the water and complains of sharks. McKisco flails away at the Mediterranean, exhausts his breath, and stands up amazed to find himself still in the shallows, just a few feet from where he began. He never understood, he admits to Rosemary, how swimmers breathe. Violet McKisco is clumsy getting up onto the raft and has to be helped by one of the tan people, Abe. In contrast to the McKiscos and Rosemary, who is "suddenly conscious of the raw whiteness of her own body," Abe

> shoved off into the water and his long body lay motionless toward shore.
>
> Rosemary and Mrs. McKisco watched him. When he had exhausted his momentum he abruptly bent double, his thin thighs rose above the surface, and he disappeared totally, leaving scarcely a fleck of foam behind.
>
> "He's a good swimmer," Rosemary said. (9)

On the raft McKisco wishes for a cigarette, but the Diver group when swimming is entirely engrossed in "the utter absorption of the swim" (21). When Abe tries to help McKisco out of his nervous funk before the duel, he says, "Do you want to take a quick dip and freshen up?" "No—no, I couldn't swim," McKisco replies (46).

It is fitting that in her transitional state Rosemary is only an intermediate swimmer. Nevertheless, she is willing to try. She got pneumonia making a picture, swimming and diving again and again all morning, though she had the grippe and fever, until Mrs. Speers put a stop to the director's retakes. Rosemary at least is ashamed of her paleness and admires good swimming. At the beach she could see that "farther up, where the beach was strewn with pebbles and dead sea-weed [where Dick had not yet done his restorative work] sat a group with flesh as white as her own. They lay under small hand parasols instead of beach umbrellas and were obviously less indigenous to the place. Between the dark people and the light, Rosemary," quite symbolically, "found room" (5–6). When she appraised the pale, poor swimmers, "she did not like these people, especially in her immediate comparison of them with those who had interested her at the other end of the beach" (8). It is also fitting, but ironically so, that when Rosemary emerges from transition she will triumph in the world of the new people, where the Babies will misapprehend everything in the most smugly oversimplified terms of black and white. Rosemary too will join the world of slugwhite people turned fashionably dark. But Diver's world, in its arrangement of parasols, mats, and sun umbrellas, is neither black nor white, but a mediation.

Dick worries about Rosemary's skin, trying to control her emergence into the brutally strong sun. He arranges "an umbrella to clip a square of sunlight off Rosemary's shoulder." Tommy's skin, on the other hand, becomes "so dark as to have lost the pleasantness of deep tan, without attaining the blue beauty of Negroes—it was just worn leather" (269). The pale people tell Rosemary, "We wanted to warn you about getting burned the first day . . . because *your* skin is important, but there seems to be so much darn formality on this beach that we didn't know whether you'd mind" (7). They are useless in preventing Rosemary from burning her legs crimson. It is by means of "formality" that Dick unremittingly struggles to manage the fine line between controlled emergence into strong new light and abandoned immersion in it, between freedom and anarchy. He creates neither the black leather of Tommy's brutal experience and hard, rapacious, sun-strong maleness nor the sickly whiteness of the new people just emerging into the sun world. He creates a fine, warm tan that is the careful, balanced order in which potentially destructive experience is regulated into a humanly usable intensity of change. He promises to buy Rosemary a sun hat to save her "reason." It is not just Nicole he guards, but, Fitzgerald uses the beach to say, the values of a world.

The protective Chinese wall against barbarism and anarchy that Dick had built on his carefully arranged beach becomes the garish home of "new paraphernalia, the trapezes over the water, the swinging rings, the portable bathhouses, the floating towers, the searchlights from last night's fetes, the modernistic buffet, white with a hackneyed motif of endless handlebars." And as for the water for good swimmers, "few people swam anymore in that blue paradise . . . —most of Gausse's guests stripped the concealing pajamas from their flabbiness only for a short hangover dip at one o'clock" (281).

Sun and Water: Hot and Cool Identities

When the critical turning point in the Divers' lives is reached in the Maria Wallis scene, as the group comes out of the station, in "the square . . . a suspended mass of gasoline exhaust cooked slowly in the July sun. It was a terrible thing—unlike pure heat it held no promise of rural escape but suggested only roads choked with the same foul asthma" (85–86). Devereux Warren's eyes are not only veined by whiskey, but are "sun-veined from rowing on Lake Geneva" (125) and are "redder than the very sun on Lake Geneva" (129). The "nothingness of the heartless beauty" of the Lake Geneva "center of the western world" (147) that the Warrens epitomize is the setting for the meeting at which Nicole will claim Dick's love as though it were her right. "It was a bright day, with sun glittering on the grass beach below and the white courts of the Kursaal. The figures on the courts threw no shadows" (147–48). Nicole's sky colored clothes and golden hair are restatements of her oneness with a golden setting in which "the thousand windows of a hotel burned in the late sun" (149). The entire funicular scene is a climb toward the sun.

The heat Diver regulates with umbrellas is too strong to take without protection. "Out there the hot light clipped close . . . [Rosemary's] shadow and she retreated—it was too bright to see. Fifty yards away the Mediterranean yielded up its pigments, moment by moment, to the brutal sunshine; below the balustrade a faded Buick cooked on the hotel drive" (4). But the colors of the sea, like those of Nicole's garden, are constantly associated with the lovely world one sees when one looks at the surfaces of the Divers' life—"a sea as mysteriously colored as the agates and cornelians of childhood, green as green milk, blue as laundry water, wine dark" (15), and in its loveliness associated with evening or early, cool morning throughout the book. (The source that lights the mysteriously colored water is not the sun: "the moon already hovered over the ruins of the aqueducts.") But when the colors of "Dicole's" life also cook and fade in the white glare with which Fitzgerald characterizes cruelly hot sunlight in this novel, Dick and Nicole appear on the corrupted beach in the black and white colors of the sun world: "The Divers went out on the beach with her white suit and his white trunks very white against the color of their bodies" (280). As the new world of hot success does to the young

Rosemary, "all dewy with belief" (34) and with "the dew . . . still on her" (4), the sun of the Barban-Warren world dries out freshness as it climbs the sky. Though all is cool and still in the fresh early morning, after the sun is well advanced "bus boys shouted in the hotel court; the dew dried upon the pines. In another hour the horns of motors began to blow down from the winding road" (3) where suspended clouds of gasoline exhaust would cook in the July sun. Noon is the high hour of the sun. "Noon dominated sea and sky—even the white line of Cannes, five miles off had faded to a mirage of what was fresh and cool," and in the deliberate symbolism with which Fitzgerald invests Dick's beach, "it seemed there was no life anywhere in all this expanse of coast except under the *filtered sunlight* of those umbrellas, where something went on amid the *color* and the murmur" and "it seemed to Rosemary that it all came from the man in the jockey cap [Dick]" (11, italics added).

Dick's concern about sunburn and umbrellas and sun hats to save sanity, his difference from both the white people and the black Barban, is his preservation of the lovely color of morally ordered life. Thus, the garden Nicole makes in the household directed by Dick is "an area so green and cool that the leaves and petals were curled with tender damp" (25). The garden flows in a "fuzzy green light" (26) and "lilac shadow" (25), "a growth of nasturtium and iris," of "kaleidoscopic peonies massed in pink clouds, black and brown tulips and fragile mauve-stemmed roses," a "scherzo of color" (26). Dick's party in the garden is set in the cool twilight and warm evening. The Divers' villa at Tarmes is in "the fresher air" (28). As the fresh young faces of the Diver children are aglow in the declining slant of "the late sunshine," Fitzgerald again introduces the name of the villa: the Villa Diana is the home where the moon is the deity, and when the children unselfconsciously sing a song with "voices . . . sweet and shrill upon the evening air" (29) to entertain the company, the song is "Au claire de la lune" (29). When Dick says farewell to Gstaad, where he feels he is saying farewell to the hopeful excitement and identity of his youth, Fitzgerald's imagery is, as always, thematically energetic:

Sun and Water: Hot and Cool Identities

> They passed the crisp green rinks where Wiener waltzes blared
> and the colors of many mountain schools flashed against the pale-
> blue skies.
> . . . Good-by, Gstaad! Good-by, fresh faces, cold sweet flow-
> ers, flakes in the darkness. Good-by, Gstaad, good-by! (179)

The book's development of Dick's dying fall is one long series of
farewells to "those illusions that give such *color* to the world." In the
scene in which Nicole, in her sun-colored dress, breaks down into mad
hostility at the fairgrounds, Fitzgerald tells us that "a high sun with a
face traced on it beat fierce on the straw hats of the children" (187).
Tommy, the sun child, is scared only when he is cold (198), but Dick
Diver's fathers and the land of his fathers are associated with a "star . . .
and a cold moon bright over Chesapeake Bay" (204). When
Rosemary's "face had changed with . . . [Dick's] looking up at it, there
was eternal moonlight in it" (211). Conversely, Nicole hears that
Tommy is in the neighborhood again "in the first hot blast of June"
(279), and the day Dick leaves his ruined beach forever is one of totally white sun glare. "A white sun, chivied of outline by a white sky,
boomed over a windless day" (311–12). Nicole and Tommy, now on
their beach, are "black and white and metallic against the sky" so white
and hot (313). The day of the showdown between Tommy, Dick, and
Nicole, like the crucial day for Gatsby at the Plaza, is one of insuffer-
able heat, with the "perfumed breeze of the fans" in the hairdressing
parlors and the coiffeuse "faintly sweating" in her "white uniform"
(307). Dick's mediation of black and white disappears, and with the
kind of "nourishment" he receives in the sun world, Dick can no
longer get his mixture of black and white, though Tommy and Nicole
get what they want. Tommy gets the demi, the blond, sun-colored
drink he orders; Nicole gets her golden summer drink, "a citron
pressé." Dick orders the "Blackenwite with siphon," but "Il n'y a plus
de Blackenwite. Nous n'avons que le Johnny Walkair" (308). All Dick
gets is an invitation to take a walk for himself, and, creating a perfect
image of the course of Diver's life, Fitzgerald has Dick's figure dimin-
ish in the dying-fall distance "until it became a dot and mingled with

the other dots in the summer crowd" (311). At this crucial point, when Dick surrenders the "happy and excited" Nicole to Tommy, Fitzgerald reinforces the fact of Dick's conscious and bitter self-sacrifice: "Nicole felt outguessed, realizing that from the episode of the camphor-rub, Dick had anticipated everything." She had the quickly fading "odd little wish that she could tell Dick all about it" (311). Even at his lowest, in miserable defeat and in consequent dependency on alcohol, Dick is worth so inestimably much more than what Carraway in *The Great Gatsby* had called "the whole rotten crowd." The summer crowd.

12

Goodbye, Dick Diver

Dick is a source of knowledge. As he used to say, "a man knows things and when he stops knowing things he's like anybody else" (162). Always "his voice promised that he would take care of . . . [one], and that a little later he would open up whole new worlds, . . . unroll an endless succession of magnificent possibilities" (16). In the things Dick does and the way he lives, one can feel "a purpose, a working over something, a direction, an act of creation different from any . . . [one has] known" (19). In his delicate and sensitive considerateness, Dick always has "his arms full of the slack he had taken up from others" (33), so that those he cares for always seem to be "still under the beach umbrella" (52), even at rambling parties in Paris.

Fitzgerald makes Dick intellectually self-conscious enough to know what makes him tick. Although deep within one part of his mind he knows that "you can't do anything about people" (78), "on the other hand, there was a pleasingness about him that simply had to be used—those who possessed that pleasingness had to keep their hands in, and go along attaching people that they had no use to make of" (87). His "trick of the heart" is both dime-store and invaluable treasure. "A part of Dick's mind was made up of the tawdry souvenirs of his boyhood. Yet in that somewhat littered Five-and-Ten, he had managed to keep alive the low painful fire of intelligence" (196). Even in his deterioration and in the heartsickness that was his self-awareness of what his life had become, Dick would bring "out all his old expertness with people, a tarnished object of art" (282).

When Dick found a "lost and miserable family of two girls and their mother" touring Europe, "an overwhelming desire to help, or to be admired, came over him: he showed them fragments of gaiety; tentatively he bought them wine, with pleasure saw them begin to regain their proper egotism" (206). Even when he is called on for help by those who have most insulted and snubbed him, "his self-knowledge assured him that he would undertake to deal with it—the old fatal pleasingness, the old forceful charm, swept back with its cry of 'Use me!'" (302). One might call Dick merely an "organizer of private gaiety, curator of a richly incrusted happiness" (76). One might call him a panderer or an impresario. One might call him a fool. There is some justice in all the appellations. But one misses the point and remains confused about Dick unless one measures him always and only within the context of moral evaluations provided by the world Fitzgerald creates in the novel. Everyone in this world is morally doomed as the old decalogues of virtues and graces are broken. Everyone except Dick uses people for selfish vanities or silly gratifications. His Americanness is the old millennial sense, the willingness of the heart to change the world, the sense of being so good, big, good, brave, good, wise, good, kind, good, grand that the vain and gorgeous self-sacrifice will be redemption. Dick is a fool, but he is a magnificent one. He is an impulsive romantic, but he is a mature and reliable healer. He is sucked into the glittering world of hot cats, but he is a man of responsibility and morality. Disintegrating though he is under the onslaught of vulgarity and selfishness with which the world responds to his cry of "Use me!" he remains the only constant moral point in a Frankenstein world of flux and change.

With the creation of the American Dr. Richard Diver, Fitzgerald brings to an apogee the American version of the dream of esteem that permeated his other novels. Having explored that need for loving esteem in *This Side of Paradise* and especially in *The Great Gatsby,* he went on in *Tender Is the Night* to dramatize the relationship of that need to the rest of the world. One might say that in his vision of the death of the America he so loved, Fitzgerald was ironically writing his deepest statement of defense of and love for America in the very novel in which Devereux Warren is the "fine American type in every way." Diver tried to dissect the "very charm" that "for Dick . . . always had an independent existence," tried to dissect "courageous grace," and, trying to "dissect it into pieces small enough to store away," realized

> that the totality of a life may be different in quality from its seg-
> ments, and also that life during one's late thirties seemed capable
> of being observed only in segments. His love for Nicole and
> Rosemary, his friendship with Abe North, with Tommy Barban in
> the broken universe of the war's ending—in such contacts the per-
> sonalities had seemed to press up so close to him that he became
> the personality itself; there seemed some necessity for taking all or
> nothing; it was as if for the remainder of his life he was con-
> demned to carry with him the egos of certain people, early met
> and early loved, and to be only as complete as they were complete
> themselves. There was some element of loneliness involved—so
> easy to be loved—so hard to love. (245)

The "lesions of vitality" that Fitzgerald described as bankruptcy in "The Crack-Up" articles are exact parallels to the waste of resources and the extravagant expenditure of self that characterize Dick. One of "his most characteristic moods" was

> the excitement that swept everyone up into it and was inevitably
> followed by his own form of melancholy. . . . This excitement
> about things reached an intensity out of proportion to their
> importance, generating a really extraordinary virtuosity with peo-
> ple. Save among a few of the tough-minded and perennially suspi-
> cious, he had the power of arousing a fascinated and uncritical
> love. The reaction came when he realized the waste and extrava-
> gance involved. (27)

Dick's pilgrimage around the block where Rosemary's studio is located—Rosemary, who was his last blooming reminder of the potential his own youth had been—is a payment of tribute to his wrenching sense of what should have been, "tribute to things unforgotten, unshriven, unexpurgated" (91). Going nowhere and running hard to keep up with Nicole's growing wealth and strength, Dick, who was going to write a great, new psychology and be the greatest psychologist who ever lived, never even finishes his small series of pamphlets.

Like Abe and his ugly drunken escapade with some blacks in Paris, Dick in his drunkenness also has an ugly moment with a black orchestra leader in a cabaret (222). Previously the darling of the Europeans, whether his peers or his servants, Dick is now to Kaethe Gregorovius "no longer a serious man" (241); and to Augustine, his drunken terror of a cook, he becomes just one more "disgusting American" (266). Even this loutish harridan can frustrate Dick and make him look clumsy. But the nadir of the debasement of the man who has become "the Black Death" and doesn't "bring people happiness any more" comes after the traumatic and dramatic fight with the cops and cabbies in Rome. Not only does Dick, who has always felt himself responsible to all humankind, come to feel a "vast criminal *irresponsibility*" (233, italics added), but to the onlooker he is no longer distinguishable from what the reader knows about Devereux Warren's real identity as incestuous pederast. As Doctor Richard Diver, child-healer, went through the courtyard to the courtroom, "a groaning, hissing, booing sound went up from the loiterers in the courtyard, voices full of fury and scorn. . . . A native of Frascati had raped and slain a five-year-old child and was to be brought in that morning—the crowd had assumed it was Dick" (234). By the end of the book Dick too wishes to hiss and boo, as earlier he had wished to be kind, to cure. His self-destructiveness and self-contempt are dramatized in his drinking; his loathing of the world that used him is dramatized in the bitter things he says, fittingly, to the likes of Lady Caroline and Mary Minghetti, and most of all to Nicole. The similarities between Dick and Abe are no longer that of Grant in the dawn of a triumphant career, no longer Lincolnesque in the democratic, egalitarian promise of a liberated new world; now the similarities exist in the painful use of words like *spic* and *smoke* and *nigger*. Daddy Dick had been father-confessor and moral guide to a world—Rosemary had felt "the smooth cloth of his dark coat like a chasuble. She seemed about to fall on her knees" (38); thinking of the Divers, Rosemary imagines them singing "a hymn, very remote in time and far away" (40). Now the healer is reduced to a spoiled priest indeed by the end of the book. The calling is gone. His last gesture is the drunken benediction of his hand raised in a papal cross above his ruined beach, a fitting symbol of the "broken universe of the war's ending" and all the broken decalogues. Dick disappears in upper New York State, which Fitzgerald used to suggest isolation and provincial lostness. The idea of American Dick fades into rumors of sordid entanglement with a girl who worked in a grocery store, of removal from small town to smaller town. Nicole "liked to think" that Dick's "career was biding its time, again like Grant's in Galena," but "in any case he is almost certainly in that section of the country, in one town or another" (315).

The dying fall of Dick is the dying fall of the promise of America and the dying fall of the book. We are left with a suffocating sense of loss and with yearning nostalgia for the idea of what Dick was to have been. Lost, gone, Fitzgerald is saying. Lost as any lost dead-end lives in lost dead-end towns. The international redeemer nation that America was to have been. In one town or another. Somewhere.

Almost certainly.

Notes

Chapter 1

1. Letter of 23 October 1940, in *The Letters of F. Scott Fitzgerald*, ed. Andrew Turnbull (New York: Charles Scribner's Sons, 1963), 128; hereafter cited in text as *Letters*.

2. For a discussion of Fitzgerald's composite characters, see Milton Stern, *The Golden Moment: The Novels of F. Scott Fitzgerald* (Urbana: University of Illinois Press, 1970); for *Tender Is the Night* especially, see pp. 289–330.

3. Riley Hughes, "F. Scott Fitzgerald: The Touch of Disaster," in *Fifty Years of the American Novel: A Christian Appraisal,* ed. Harold C. Gardiner (New York: Charles Scribner's Sons, 1951), 135–49.

4. See James Thurber's recollections in *Credos and Curios* (New York: Harper & Row, 1962), 159; see also Fitzgerald's important letter to John Peale Bishop, 7 April 1934, *Letters,* 363.

5. There have been several discussions of Spenglerian patterns of history in Fitzgerald's work. Two especially useful commentaries are Richard Lehan, *F. Scott Fitzgerald and the Craft of Fiction* (Carbondale: Southern Illinois University Press, 1966), and Joan Kirkby, "Spengler and Apocalyptic Typology in F. Scott Fitzgerald's *Tender Is the Night,*" *Southern Review* (Australia) 12 (November 1979): 246–61.

6. An excellent study of this aspect of *Tender Is the Night* and of Fitzgerald's work generally is John F. Callahan, *The Illusions of a Nation: Myth and History in the Novels of F. Scott Fitzgerald* (Urbana: University of Illinois Press, 1972).

Chapter 2

1. Quoted by Malcolm Cowley in his introduction to the revised edition of *Tender Is the Night,* in *Three Novels of F. Scott Fitzgerald,* ed. Malcolm Cowley (New York: Charles Scribner's Sons, 1953), v; hereafter cited in the text.

2. Alexander Cowie, *The Rise of the American Novel* (New York: American Book Co., 1948), 747.

3. Arthur Mizener, "F. Scott Fitzgerald, 1896–1940: The Poet of Borrowed Time," in *Lives of Eighteen from Princeton,* ed. Willard Thorp (Princeton, N.J.: Princeton University Press, 1946), 333–53.

4. Arthur Mizener, ed. *F. Scott Fitzgerald: A Collection of Critical Essays* (Englewood Cliffs, N.J.: Prentice Hall, 1963).

5. D. W. Harding, "Mechanisms of Misery," *Scrutiny* 3 (December 1934): 316–19.

6. Kenneth E. Eble, ed., *F. Scott Fitzgerald: A Collection of Criticism* (New York: McGraw-Hill, 1973).

7. Marvin J. LaHood, ed., *"Tender Is the Night": Essays in Criticism* (Bloomington: Indiana University Press, 1969).

8. Philip Rahv, "You Can't Duck Hurricane under a Beach Umbrella," *Daily Worker,* 5 May 1934, 7.

9. Matthew Bruccoli, *The Composition of "Tender Is the Night"* (Pittsburgh: University of Pittsburgh Press, 1963). Bruccoli's book is the definitive study of the manuscripts of the novel in its various stages. Facsimiles of the manuscripts are provided in the *Tender Is the Night* volumes (numbers 4a,I; 4a,II; 4b,I; 4b,II; 4b,III; 4b,IV; and 4b,V) of Bruccoli's edition of *F. Scott Fitzgerald Manuscripts* (New York and London: Garland, 1990–91), 18 vols.

10. Charles Poore, "Books of the Times," *New York Times,* 15 November 1951, 27: "When *Tender Is the Night* was first published in 1934 some (but by no means all) critics were haring hotly after proletarian novels, the wild-westerns of the intellectuals. They looked sternly down their noses at Fitzgerald's story of the heart's splendor. Others used it as a stick to beat the expatriates. It would be preposterous, however, to think that was the reason for *Tender Is the Night*'s failure to be an immense success. The public spent its shrinking dollars even more sparingly on the Ph.D.'s to-the-barricades novels. In 1934 it was reading Stark Young's *So Red the Rose* and James Hilton's *Good-Bye, Mr. Chips* in quantities."

11. Matthew Bruccoli, *"Tender Is the Night*—Reception and Reputation," *Profile of F. Scott Fitzgerald,* ed. Bruccoli (Columbus, Ohio: Charles E. Merrill Publishing Co., 1971), 93–94. The essay (pp. 92–106) is a revision of pp. 1–16 of Bruccoli's *The Composition of "Tender Is the Night."*

12. There are rich bibliographical aids for a study of the reception of *Tender Is the Night.* As Bruccoli is the primary textual scholar and discoverer and compiler of facts and memorabilia concerning Fitzgerald, Jackson Bryer is the primary bibliographer of Fitzgerald scholarship and criticism. See Bryer's *The Critical Reputation of F. Scott Fitzgerald: A Bibliographical Study* (Hamden, Conn.: Archon Books, 1967); his *Supplement One through 1981* to *The Critical Reputation* (Archon, 1984); his *F. Scott Fitzgerald: The Critical*

Reception (New York: Burt Franklin & Co., 1978); and his "Four Decades of Fitzgerald Studies: The Best and the Brightest," *Twentieth Century Literature* 26 (Summer 1980): 247–67. See also Milton R. Stern, ed., *Critical Essays on F. Scott Fitzgerald's "Tender Is the Night"* (Boston: G. K. Hall, 1986); hereafter cited in text as *Critical Essays*.

13. Amy Loveman, for instance, in her article on the spring list of new books for the influential *Saturday Review*, spared only two sentences for *Tender Is the Night*, concluding that "it is not a good novel" (*Saturday Review of Literature*, 7 April 1934, 610).

14. C. Hartley Grattan, review of *Tender Is the Night*, *Modern Monthly* 8 (July 1934): 375–77.

15. Letter of 26 September 1934, in *Correspondence of F. Scott Fitzgerald*, ed. Matthew Bruccoli and Margaret M. Duggan (New York: Random House, 1980), 368; hereafter cited in text as *Correspondence*.

16. Bruccoli comments in *"Tender Is the Night*—Reception and Reputation": "The critic who finds Dick Diver an unconvincing or confusing character will not be persuaded otherwise by any amount of argument—or by a detailed reconstruction of the composition of *Tender Is the Night*. For the record, this reader believes that Dick Diver is a satisfying character, that the causes of his deterioration are sufficiently probed, that his fall is moving, and that the novel is unified by Fitzgerald's view of his hero. A study of the manuscripts supports some of these beliefs. Although Fitzgerald did not write long, detailed analyses of his work, the preliminary sketch of Dick Diver prepared in 1932 indicates that he knew the causes of Dick's decline. The first holograph draft for the published version of *Tender Is the Night* reveals that Fitzgerald felt he thoroughly understood his hero" (101).

17. See the concluding paragraph of Cowley's introduction to *Three Novels of F. Scott Fitzgerald*.

18. For an introduction to the problem, see the section on "The Text Itself" in Stern, *Critical Essays*, 21–57.

19. In either version structure does not create a problem for meaning. As Bruccoli asserts, "Readers recognized that the revised structure did not really have a significant effect on the essential qualities of *Tender Is the Night*" (*"Tender Is the Night*—Reception and Reputation," 99). Bruccoli argues that if there is confusion in the novel, it results from chronology rather than structure. See "Material for a Centenary Edition of *Tender Is the Night*," in Stern, *Critical Essays*, 32–57.

20. Early in the decade Oscar Cargill's unfavorable and ignorant review was typical; see *Intellectual America* (New York: Macmillan, 1941), 342–46, esp. 344. In 1943 Maxwell Geismar thought *Tender Is the Night* a good book badly focused; see *The Last of the Provincials* (Boston: Houghton Mifflin), 327–37. J. Donald Adams thought it was a bad novel; see *The Shape of Books*

to Come (New York: Viking Press, 1944), 89–90. Arthur Mizener said that the novel was Fitzgerald's best; see "The Poet of Borrowed Time," in Thorpe's 1946 *Lives of Eighteen from Princeton*. Theodore Adams's essay, "A Noble Issue," in *Gifthorse* (Columbus: Ohio State University, 1949), 35–43, was adumbratively perceptive, and, significantly, appeared at the *end* of the decade.

21. John Berryman, "F. Scott Fitzgerald," *Kenyon Review* 8 (Winter 1946): 107.

22. Arthur Mizener, "The Portable F. Scott Fitzgerald," *Kenyon Review* 8 (Spring 1946): 342.

23. Arnold Gingrich, "Salute and Farewell to F. Scott Fitzgerald," *Esquire,* March 1941, 6. It is moving to see that one of Fitzgerald's Pat Hobby stories runs in the same issue.

24. Stephen Vincent Benét, "Fitzgerald's Unfinished Symphony," *Saturday Review of Literature,* 6 December 1941, 10.

25. *Tender Is the Night,* ed. Malcolm Cowley (New York: Scribner's, 1951).

26. Arthur Mizener, *The Far Side of Paradise* (Boston: Houghton Mifflin, 1951).

27. *The Crack-Up,* ed. Edmund Wilson (New York: New Directions, 1945).

28. Alfred Kazin, ed., *F. Scott Fitzgerald: The Man and His Work* (New York: World Publishing Co., 1951).

29. James E. Miller, *The Fictional Technique of Scott Fitzgerald* (The Hague: Martinus Nijhoff, 1957).

30. Kingsley Amis, "The Crack-Up," (London) *Spectator,* 20 November 1959, 719.

31. Anonymous, "Power without Glory," (London) *Times Literary Supplement,* 20 January 1950, 40.

32. Leslie Fiedler, "Notes on F. Scott Fitzgerald," *New Leader,* 16 April 1951, 23–24.

33. Kazin, introduction to *F. Scott Fitzgerald: The Man and His Work.*

34. John Aldridge, *After the Lost Generation* (New York: McGraw-Hill, 1951), 52–55.

35. A. H. Steinberg, "Fitzgerald's Portrait of a Psychiatrist," *University of Kansas City Review* 21 (March 1955): 219–22.

36. Dan Jacobson, "F. Scott Fitzgerald," *Encounter* 14 (June 1960): 71–77.

37. John R. Kuehl, "Scott Fitzgerald: Romantic and Realist," *Texas Studies in Literature and Language* 1 (Autumn 1959): 412–26.38.

Notes

38. Richard Schoenwald, "F. Scott Fitzgerald as John Keats," *Boston University Studies in English* 3 (Spring 1957): 12–21. See also William E. Doherty, *"Tender Is the Night* and the 'Ode to a Nightingale,'" in *Explorations of Literature,* ed. Rima Drell Reck (Baton Rouge: Louisiana State University Press, 1966), 100–114. Although authoring an excellent essay, Doherty incorrectly claims that no previous attention had been paid to the subject.

39. George D. Murphy, "The Unconscious Dimension of *Tender Is the Night,"* *Studies in the Novel* 5 (Fall 1975): 314. Unfortunately, Murphy devotes the rest of his essay to a dismissal of the "socioeconomic" dimensions of the book in a revelation of the "real" psychological motivation, which becomes a formulaic reduction of *Tender Is the Night* to an allegory of the relation of the son (Dick, the ego) to the fathers (*all* the fathers, the superego).

40. In tandem with the Doherty essay (see note 38), James W. Tuttleton's "Vitality and Vampirism in *Tender Is the Night"* (in Stern, *Critical Essays*) is instructive. The best example of the repudiation of Diver's idealism is Callahan's *The Illusions of a Nation.*

41. The heavy ideologizing in the late 1960s and early 1970s, announcing the cultural issues that would dominate the rest of the century, had not yet developed the more balanced perspectives that mark later and more sophisticated ideological criticism. Madonna C. Kolbenschlag, for instance, asserted that "Fitzgerald, mystified by the competitive and erratic 'animus' of Zelda, seems also to have failed to fully comprehend the dimensions of 'anima' in himself—in effect, he never successfully demythologized the sexual stereotypes of masculinity and femininity in his sensibility." By implication, the dimension and center of *Tender Is the Night* are Fitzgerald's sexist creation of sexual stereotypes. See "Madness and Sexual Mythology in Scott Fitzgerald," *International Journal of Women's Studies* 1 (May–June 1978): 270. Following an earlier lead from Leslie Fiedler, who in effect exonerates the Warren world by making Nicole a victim of Dick ("Some Notes on F. Scott Fitzgerald," in *An End to Innocence: Essays on Culture and Politics* [Boston: Beacon Press, 1955], 174–82), Milton Hindus ignores the novel's stated facts and goes so far as to assume that Nicole was never raped by Daddy, that it was all in her mind, and that Dick was a sexually stupid psychiatrist foolish enough to believe her; see *F. Scott Fitzgerald: An Introduction and an Interpretation* (New York: Holt, Rinehart & Winston, 1968), 50–69.

42. Henry Dan Piper, "F. Scott Fitzgerald and the Image of His Father," (Princeton University) *Library Chronicle* 12 (Summer 1951): 181–86.

43. Although varying widely in the degree to which they might be called "Marxist," some typical examples from the 1980s are Ronald J. Gervais, "The Socialist and the Silk Stockings: Fitzgerald's Double Allegiance," *Mosaic* 15, no. 2 (1982): 79–92; Michael Spindler, *American Literature and Social Change: William Dean Howells to Arthur Miller* (Bloomington: Indiana

University Press, 1983); and Richard Godden, "Money Makes Manners Make Man Make Woman: *Tender Is the Night,* a Familiar Romance?" *Literature and History* 12 (1968): 16–37.

44. Perhaps the best of these is Ruth Prigozy's excellent "From Griffith's Girls to *Daddy's Girl:* The Masks of Innocence in *Tender Is the Night,"* *Twentieth Century Literature* 26 (1980): 189–221. Other examples include Lindel Ryan, "F. Scott Fitzgerald and the Battle of the Sexes," *Literature in North Queensland* 8, no. 3 (1980): 84–94; Mary A. McCoy, "Fitzgerald's Women: Beyond Winter Dreams," *American Novelists Revisited* (Boston: G. K. Hall, 1983); Judith Fetterley, "Who Killed Dick Diver? The Sexual Politics of *Tender Is the Night,"* *Mosaic* 17, no. 1 (1984): 111–28; and Sarah Beebe Fryer, *Fitzgerald's New Women: Harbingers of Change* (Ann Arbor, Mich.: UMI Research Press, 1988).

45. See, for example, Sarah B. Fryer, "Nicole Warren Diver and Alabama Beggs Knight: Women on the Threshold of Freedom," *Modern Fiction Studies* 31 (1985): 318–25.

46. Gene D. Phillips, S.J., *Fiction, Film, and F. Scott Fitzgerald* (Chicago: Loyola University Press, 1986), and Wheeler Winston Dixon, *The Cinematic Vision of F. Scott Fitzgerald* (Ann Arbor, Mich.: UMI Research Press, 1986), are two examples of the continuing interest in Fitzgerald and the movies.

47. "Standard" topics not representing any particular ideology are typified in Joan Kirkby's "Spengler and Apocalyptic Typology in F. Scott Fitzgerald's *Tender Is the Night"* and Robert Merrill's *"Tender Is the Night* as a Tragic Action," *Texas Studies in Language and Literature* 25 (1983): 597–615.

48. For full citations on Stern and Bryer, see note 12; *American Literary Scholarship* (Durham, N.C.: Duke University Press, ongoing).

Chapter 3

1. Fitzgerald's "General Plan" for the book is given in full as appendix B in Mizener's *The Far Side of Paradise.*

2. 23 April 1934, *Letters,* 510. Fitzgerald discusses the dying fall in a letter to John Peale Bishop, 7 April 1934, *Letters,* 363. See also his letters on the subject to Ernest Hemingway, 1 June 1934, *Letters,* 309–10, and to John O'Hara, 25 July 1936, *Letters,* 538.

3. From the journal of Laura Guthrie, quoted in Andrew Turnbull, *Scott Fitzgerald* (New York: Scribner's, 1962), 259; hereafter cited in text.

Chapter 4

1. It should be clear that my use of the term *romantic* follows Fitzgerald's and is not an attempt at the precise genus *Romantic,* which in itself

is vexingly protean and amorphous. Fitzgerald's usage contains in part the philosophical idealism of Romantic epistemology and ontology. But even though there are some essential similarities between the two terms, Fitzgerald's is simpler and even less precise. He uses the word in a popular—not a scholarly, historical, or philosophical—sense. He aims at a category of emotion, imagination, and sensibility. He means the person with bedroom eyes, the person who wants to be popular, of course; but that is a small and the least important part, a surface aspect, of Fitzgerald's use of *romantic*. Most largely and centrally he means the dreamer with a heightened sensitivity to the promises of life, the individual whose temperament is attuned to what he called those illusions whose color give life a magical glory. He means Gatsby. He means Diver. He means himself.

Chapter 8

1. "Early Success," *American Cavalcade,* October 1937; reprinted in *The Crack-Up,* ed. Edmund Wilson (New York: New Directions, 1945), 89–90; the essay is hereafter cited in text.

Selected Bibliography

Not all works mentioned in the endnotes are repeated in this brief bibliography. The combination of bibliography and endnotes will give the student a glimpse of the chronological and ideological range of Fitzgerald criticism and provide a beginning place for the new researcher and the seriously interested reader.

Primary Sources

Tender Is the Night. New York: Charles Scribner's Sons, 1934.

Tender Is the Night. New York: Charles Scribner's Sons, 1962.

Tender Is the Night. Edited by Malcolm Cowley. New York: Charles Scribner's Sons, 1951.

See "Note on the References and Acknowledgments."

Secondary Sources
Books and Parts of Books

Allen, Joan M. *Candles and Carnival Lights: The Catholic Sensibility of F. Scott Fitzgerald*. New York: New York University Press, 1978.

Bruccoli, Matthew J. *The Composition of "Tender Is the Night": A Study of the Manuscripts*. Pittsburgh: University of Pittsburgh Press, 1963.

_____, ed. *As Ever, Scott Fitz—: Letters between F. Scott Fitzgerald and His Literary Agent Harold Ober: 1919–1940*. Philadelphia and New York: J. B. Lippincott Co., 1972.

_____. *The Notebooks of F. Scott Fitzgerald*. New York and London: Harcourt Brace Jovanovich, 1979.

_____, and Margaret M. Duggan, eds. *Correspondence of F. Scott Fitzgerald*. New York: Random House, 1980.

_____. "Material for a Centenary Edition of *Tender Is the Night*. In *Critical Essays on F. Scott Fitzgerald's "Tender Is the Night,"* edited by Milton R. Stern, 32–57. Boston: G. K. Hall, 1986.

Bryer, Jackson R. *The Critical Reputation of F. Scott Fitzgerald: A Bibliographical Study*. Hamden, Conn.: Archon Books, 1967.

_____. *The Critical Reputation of F. Scott Fitzgerald: Supplement One Through 1981*. Hamden, Conn.: Archon Books, 1984.

Callahan, John F. *The Illusions of a Nation: Myth and History in the Novels of F. Scott Fitzgerald*. Urbana: University of Illinois Press, 1972.

Cowley, Malcolm. Introduction to *Tender Is the Night*. In *Three Novels of F. Scott Fitzgerald*, edited by Malcolm Cowley, iii–xii. New York: Charles Scribner's Sons, 1953.

Chambers, John B. *The Novels of F. Scott Fitzgerald*. New York: St. Martin's Press, 1989.

Donaldson, Scott. *Fool for Love*. New York: Congdon & Weed, 1983.

_____. "A Short History of *Tender Is the Night*." In *Writing the American Classics*, edited by James Barbour and Tom Quirk, 177–208. Chapel Hill: University of North Carolina Press, 1990.

Eble, Kenneth E., ed. *F. Scott Fitzgerald: A Collection of Criticism*. New York: McGraw-Hill, 1973.

Fussell, Edwin. "Fitzgerald's Brave New World." In *The Great Gatsby: A Study*, edited by Frederick J. Hoffman, 244–62. New York: Charles Scribner's Sons, 1962.

Kinahan, Frank. "Focus on F. Scott Fitzgerald's *Tender Is the Night*." In *American Dreams, American Nightmares*, edited by David Madden, 115–28. Carbondale: Southern Illinois University Press, 1970.

Kuehl, John, and Jackson R. Bryer, eds. *Dear Scott/Dear Max: The Fitzgerald-Perkins Correspondence*. New York: Charles Scribner's Sons, 1971.

LaHood, Marvin J., ed. *"Tender Is the Night": Essays in Criticism*. Bloomington and London: Indiana University Press, 1969.

Lehan, Richard D. *F. Scott Fitzgerald and the Craft of Fiction*. Carbondale: Southern Illinois University Press, 1966.

Le Vot, André. *F. Scott Fitzgerald: A Biography*. Translated by William Byron. Garden City, N.Y.: Doubleday and Co., 1983.

Mellow, James. *Invented Lives*. Boston: Houghton Mifflin, 1984.

Miller, James E., Jr. *F. Scott Fitzgerald: His Art and His Technique*. New York: New York University Press, 1964.

Mizener, Arthur. "F. Scott Fitzgerald, 1896–1940: The Poet of Borrowed Time." In *Lives of Eighteen from Princeton*, edited by Willard Thorp, 333–53. Princeton, N.J.: Princeton University Press, 1946.

Selected Bibliography

_____. *The Far Side of Paradise.* Boston: Houghton Mifflin, 1951.

_____. "*Tender Is the Night.*" In *Twelve Great American Novels,* 104–19. New York: New American Library, 1967.

Perosa, Sergio. *The Art of F. Scott Fitzgerald.* Translated by Charles Matz and Sergio Perosa. Ann Arbor: University of Michigan Press, 1965.

Sklar, Robert. *F. Scott Fitzgerald: The Last Laocoon.* New York: Oxford University Press, 1967.

Stavola, Thomas J. *Scott Fitzgerald: Crisis in an American Identity.* New York: Barnes & Noble Books, 1979.

Stern, Milton R. *The Golden Moment: The Novels of F. Scott Fitzgerald.* Urbana: University of Illinois Press, 1970.

_____. *Critical Essays on F. Scott Fitzgerald's "Tender Is the Night."* Boston: G. K. Hall, 1986.

Trachtenberg, Alan. "The Journey Back: Myth and History in *Tender Is the Night.*" In *Experience in the Novel: Selected Papers from the English Institute,* edited by Roy Harvey Pearce, 133–62. New York: Columbia University Press, 1968.

Turnbull, Andrew. *Scott Fitzgerald.* New York: Charles Scribner's Sons, 1962.

_____. *The Letters of Scott Fitzgerald.* New York: Charles Scribner's Sons, 1963.

Way, Brian. *F. Scott Fitzgerald and the Art of Social Fiction.* New York: St. Martin's Press, 1980.

Wenke, Joseph. "*Tender Is the Night:* A Cross-referenced Bibliography of Criticism." In *Critical Essays on F. Scott Fitzgerald's "Tender Is the Night,"* edited by Milton R. Stern, 247–69. Boston: G. K. Hall, 1986.

Wilson, Edmund, ed. *The Crack Up.* New York: New Directions, 1945.

Journal Articles

Coleman, Tom C. III. "The Rise of Dr. Diver." *Discourse* 13 (Spring 1970): 226–38.

_____. "Nicole Warren Diver and Scott Fitzgerald: The Girl and the Egotist." *Studies in the Novel* 3 (Spring 1971): 34–43.

Donaldson, Scott. "'No, I am Not Prince Charming': Fairy Tales in *Tender Is the Night.*" *Fitzgerald/Hemingway Annual* 5 (1973): 105–12.

Fetterley, Judith. "Who Killed Dick Diver? The Sexual Politics of *Tender Is the Night.*" *Mosaic* 17, no. 1 (1984): 111–28.

Foster, Richard. "Time's Exile: Dick Diver and the Heroic Idea." *Mosaic* 8 (Spring 1975): 89–108.

Fryer, Sarah B. "Nicole Warren Diver and Alabama Beggs Knight: Women on the Threshold of Freedom." *Modern Fiction Studies* 31 (1985): 318–25.

Grenberg, Bruce L. "Fitzgerald's 'Figured Curtain': Personality and History in *Tender Is the Night.*" *Fitzgerald/Hemingway Annual 1978* (1979): 105–36.

Hall, William F. "Dialogue and Theme in *Tender Is the Night.*" *Modern Language Notes* 76 (November 1961): 616–22.

Higgins, Brian, and Hershel Parker. "Sober Second Thoughts: Fitzgerald's 'Final Version'" of *Tender Is the Night.*" *Proof* 4 (1975): 129–52.

Kallich, Martin. "F. Scott Fitzgerald: Money or Morals." *University of Kansas City Review* 15 (Summer 1949): 271–80.

Kirkby, Joan. "Spengler and Apocalyptic Typology in F. Scott Fitzgerald's *Tender Is the Night.*" *Southern Review: Literary and Disciplinary Essays* 12, no. 3 (November 1979): 246–61.

Light, James F. "Political Conscience in the Novels of F. Scott Fitzgerald." *Ball State Teacher's College Forum* 4 (Spring 1963): 13–25.

McNichols, Sr. Mary Verity. "Fitzgerald's Women in *Tender Is the Night.*" *College Literature* 4 (Winter 1977): 40–70.

Merrill, Robert. "*Tender Is the Night* as a Tragic Action." *Texas Studies in Literature and Language* 25 (1983): 597–615.

Prigozy, Ruth. "From Griffith's Girls to *Daddy's Girl:* The Masks of Innocence in *Tender Is the Night.*" *Twentieth Century Literature* 26 (Summer 1980): 189–221.

Roulston, Robert. "Dick Diver's Plunge into the Roman Void: The Setting of *Tender Is the Night.*" *South Atlantic Quarterly* 77 (Winter 1978): 85–97.

Schoenwald, Richard L. "F. Scott Fitzgerald as John Keats." *Boston University Studies in English* 3 (Spring 1957): 12–21.

Stanton, Robert. "'Daddy's Girl': Symbol and Theme in *Tender Is the Night.*" *Modern Fiction Studies* 4 (Summer 1958): 136–42.

Stark, John. "The Style of *Tender Is the Night.*" *Fitzgerald/ Hemingway Annual* 4 (1972): 89–95.

Steinberg, A. H. "Fitzgerald's Portrait of a Psychiatrist." *University of Kansas City Review* 21 (March 1955): 219–22.

Toles, George. "The Metaphysics of Style in *Tender Is the Night.*" *American Literature* 62 (1990): 423–44.

Wasserstrom, William. "The Strange Case of F. Scott Fitzgerald and A. Hyd(Hid)ell: A Note on the Displaced Person in American Life and Literature." *Columbia University Forum* 8 (Fall 1965): 5–11.

West, Suzanne. "Nicole's Gardens." *Fitzgerald/Hemingway Annual* 10 (1978): 85–95.

Wexelblatt, Robert. "*Tender Is the Night* and History." *Essays in Literature* (Western Illinois University) 17 (1990): 232–41.

Index

Index

Index

Poore, Charles, 16, 134n10
"Power without Glory," 136n31
Prangins Clinic, xii
Prigozy, Ruth, 138n44
Princeton University, ix, x
Private Worlds, 16
Psychiatric Congress, 96

Rahv, Philip, 16, 134n8
Real, Señor Pardo y Ciudad, 40–42, 112
Reck, Rima Drell, 137n38
Richard Diver, xiv
The Rise of the American Novel, 134n2
The Romantic Egotist, x
the Russian Revolution, 9, 13
Ryan, Lindel, 138n44

St. Paul, Minnesota, ix, xi, xi
St. Paul Academy, ix
Salinger, J. D., 12
"Salute and Farewell to F. Scott Fitzgerald," 136n23
Saturday Evening Post, x, xi, xii, xiii
Saturday Review of Literature, 17, 135n13, 136n24
Save Me the Waltz, xii
Schoenwald, Richard, 23, 137n38
Schulberg, Budd, xiii
Scott Fitzgerald, 138n3
"Scott Fitzgerald: Romantic and Realist," 136n37
Scribner's, Charles and Sons, x
Scribner's Magazine, xiv
Seven Gothic Tales, 16
The Shape of Books to Come, 135–36n20
Sheppard-Pratt Hospital, xii
Sibley-Biers, Lady Caroline, 49, 58, 67–68, 72, 88, 106, 130
Smart Set, x

"The Socialist and the Silk Stockings," 137n43
"Some Notes on F. Scott Fitzgerald," 137n41
So Red the Rose, 16, 134n10
Speers, Mrs. Elsie, 56; and Dick Divers, 80–82, 93
Spengler, Oswald, and Spenglerisim, 8, 9, 11, 13, 135n5, 138n47
"Spengler and Apocalyptic Typology in F. Scott Fitzgerald's *Tender Is the Night*," 133n5, 138n47
Spindler, Michael, 137n43
Steinberg, A. H., 136n35
Stern, Milton, R., vii, viii, 28, 133n2, 135n12, 135n18, 135n19, 137n40, 138n48
stock market crash, xii
Studies in the Novel, 137n39
"The Swimmer," 5
Syracuse, New York, ix

Tales of the Jazz Age, xi
Talmadge, Norma, 118
Taps at Reveille, xii
Tender Is the Night: and America and Europe, 88–97, 101–3; as American historical novel, 12, 26; and anarchy, 41, 49, 50; begun, xi; biographical and historical context, 11, 13; category of fiction, 37; and charm, 36–37; and composite characters, 9–11; critical reception of, 14–28 (in the 1930s, 15–19; in the 1960s and 1970s, 23–26; in the 1980s and 1990s, 26–28); *Daddy's Girl* and daddy's girl, 40–41; dedication, xi; and disease, 31; and disillusion in *The Great Gatsby,* 84–85; and the dying fall, 31–33, 37, 50, 117,

Index

The Author

Milton R. Stern is a Distinguished Alumni Professor Emeritus of the University of Connecticut, where he was a member of the English Department for 33 years. He has taught at Michigan State University, Harvard University, the University of Wyoming, Smith College, the University of Illinois, and, as a Fulbright Professor of American Literature, at the University of Warsaw, Poland. He was a founder and chairman of the Connecticut Humanities Council of the State Based Programs of the National Endowment for the Humanities and has lectured widely on the humanities in the United States. Professor Stern has been the recipient of a grant from the American Council of Learned Societies, has been a fellow of the National Endowment for the Humanities National Humanities Institute at Yale University, and has been a Guggenheim fellow. He has published several articles and reviews, and his books include *The Fine Hammered Steel of Herman Melville*; *The Golden Moment: The Novels of F. Scott Fitzgerald,* the Viking Portable *American Literature Survey,* with S. L. Gross, *Critical Essays on Herman Melville's "Typee,"* *Critical Essays on F. Scott Fitzgerald's "Tender Is the Night,"* and *Contexts for Hawthorne.*